WORDS IN ACTION

The 5 C's Approach to Good Writing

John McGuire
St. Ambrose College

UNIVERSITY
PRESS OF
AMERICA

LANHAM • NEW YORK • LONDON

Copyright © 1984 by

John F. McGuire

University Press of America,™ Inc.

4720 Boston Way
Lanham, MD 20706

3 Henrietta Street
London WC2E 8LU England

All rights reserved

Printed in the United States of America

Library of Congress Cataloging in Publication Data

McGuire, John F.
   Words in action.

   Includes index.
   1. English language–Rhetoric. 2. English language –
Business English. I. Title.
PE1479.B87M37 1984   808'.042   84–5182
ISBN 0–8191–3951–3 (alk. paper)
ISBN 0–8191–3952–1 (pbk. : alk. paper)

This textbook uses neuter language, where possible.
In other contexts the words "he," "his," "him," represent
both masculine and feminine genders.

FOR   Betty
       and
    Ryan and Kelly

PERFORMANCE GOALS FOR <u>WORDS IN ACTION</u> COURSE

This course should help students improve in the following areas:

1. Write a letter, memo, or report with a clear realization of its purpose.

2. Realize the important role of communications in the success of an organization.

3. Write clearly and concisely by using the purpose statement as the primary guideline.

4. Follow a coherent organizational plan for letters, memos, and reports.

5. Choose clear, concrete, and specific words.

6. Write paragraphs that follow a clear design and include coherent transitions.

7. Make an informed choice among the patterns of development for reports.

8. Make statements recognizable by the reader as facts, inferences, or judgments.

9. Use a sincere, human tone in correspondence.

10. Express ideas in language generally accepted as correct usage.

Table of Contents

PART ONE -- Principles of Successful Communication 1- 1

    Chapter One -- A Start 1- 1

        A Key Word -- Purpose 1- 2

        What's Your Attitude About Language? 1- 2

        What About Speed-Writing? 1- 4

        The Time and Place for Good Writing 1- 5

        Steps in the Writing Process 1- 6

        Exercises 1- 8

        Applications 1-14

    Chapter Two -- Communication Theory 2- 1

        Communication and Performance 2- 1

        What Price Communication? 2- 1

        Real World vs. Word World 2- 2

        The Abstraction Process 2- 5

        Denotation and Connotation 2- 8

        Objective Writing 2-10

        Applications 2-12

PART TWO -- The Five C's of Good Writing 3- 1

    Chapter Three -- Good Writing Is Clear 3- 1

        Use Concrete Terms 3- 2

        Use Specific Terms 3- 4

        Clarify Your Purpose 3- 5

        Eliminate Jargon 3- 6

        Does Shortness Guarantee Clarity? 3- 8

    Use of "Fad" words 3- 8

    Readability Formulas 3-10

    Fog Index Formula 3-10

    A Final Test for Clarity 3-12

    A Transition 3-13

    Exercises 3-14

    Applications 3-20

Chapter Four -- Good Writing Is Concise 4- 1

    Try This Revision Method 4- 2

    Reduce Verbiage 4- 2

    Use Short Words 4- 3

    Use "Working" Verbs 4- 4

    Break Down Elements to Simpler Forms 4- 6

    Avoid Redundancy 4- 9

    Nouns as Modifiers 4-11

    Avoid Euphemisms and Inflated Language 4-11

    Drop Cliches 4-13

    Exercises 4-16

Chapter Five -- Good Writing Is Coherent 5- 1

    English as an Analytical (Position) Language 5- 1

    Order of Sentence Units 5- 2

    Use of Connective Words 5- 3

    Sentence Patterns for Coherence 5- 4

    Coherence of the Paragraph 5-10

    Lists of Transitional Words 5-12

    The Transitional Paragraph 5-13

    Patterns of Coherence in the Report 5-14

    Four Steps in Developing a Coherent Report 5-21

    Exercises 5-28

Chapter Six -- Good Writing Is Considerate 6- 1

    The YOU Attitude 6- 1

    Facts-Inferences-Judgments 6- 3

    Watch Intensives and Hedgers 6- 7

    Avoid Logical Fallacies 6- 8

    Choose Positive Over Negative Expression 6-11

    Watch "Relative" Words 6-13

    Exercises 6-14

Chapter Seven -- Good Writing Is Correct 7- 1

    Is Some Modern Fiction Ungrammatical? 7- 2

    What About the Purist View? 7- 2

    Levels of Usage for Written English 7- 4

    Does Your Bad Grammar Show? 7- 5

    Common Usage Problems 7- 6

        Does your sentence go far enough
        or too far 7- 6

        Are you right on "time"? 7- 7

        Are you a good match-maker in your
        sentence? 7-10

        Whom do you want? 7-11

        Have you forgotten the apostrophe? 7-13

        Are you real (or really) confident about
        your English? 7-15

How about your signals (punctuation)?	7-16
How is your spelling?	7-20
Words Commonly Confused	7-23
Exercises	7-30
Postscript	A
Index	B
Acknowledgements	C

A START

CHAPTER 1

PART ONE

Chapter One--A Start

Objectives of Chapter One:

1. To introduce the concept of PURPOSE in writing.

2. To analyze the writer's purpose and attitudes.

3. To explain four steps in a writing plan.

Goethe: "If you treat a man as he is, he will remain as he is. If you treat him as if he were what he could and should be, he will become what he could and should be."

    Any course of instruction should emphasize such an educational principle at its very beginning. Instruction in any field presupposes the need for change--in attitudes, techniques, or approaches to one's job duties. And, following the instruction, the assumption is that these changes will carry over into an employee's performance.

    This text presents the Five C's approach--good writing is CLEAR, CONCISE, COHERENT, CONSIDERATE, and CORRECT--and is a product of the author's three decades of experience in teaching composition and communications courses. The material is designed to make the course practical for college students and those already working in business or government positions. Since too many texts on written composition suffer from a hide-bound, too-theoretical approach, the text contains almost no heavy, Latinized grammar terms that more often confuse rather than help the student. The emphasis is on good usage rather than the rules--on positive steps to make writing better rather than memorizing terms and rules to avoid mistakes. This revised edition of Words in Action introduces many changes suggested by more than five hundred students who have studied from the original 1976 edition.

    The course you are undertaking exists to help you improve your techniques in written communication. The training, however, should do more than that--the principles learned here should also carry over into better speaking and listening skills. To assure this, efforts have been made to make the text and hand-outs of practical use to you. Try as soon as possible and as far as possible to use the training in your writing performance. If you begin now, good techniques may have already become a matter of habit by the time the course ends. Improvement will come to those who want to improve.

A Key Word

The first key word for this course is PURPOSE. You will be tired of hearing the word repeated through the text and class sessions, but if you understand its relevance to your own writing, a great lesson will be learned. The key question related to purpose is WHY? Why am I writing this memo, report, or letter? What is it supposed to accomplish? What is the reader to learn from it, to do as a result of reading it? If you cannot come up with an answer to the question "WHY?" perhaps you can save yourself a great deal of work. Is there too much emphasis on producing writing merely for its own sake? Do people feel motivated to fill the filing cabinets because they are there? If there are no better reasons than these, don't write it--and save some small part of the reams of paper already inundating business and government today. Someone with a perceptive mind said it in the form of the Ninth Beatitude:

> Blessed be the man who having nothing to say abstains from giving evidence of this in words.

Isn't that worth thinking about?

Let us take the long view of this word "purpose" and speak in general of the reasons for and the result of most of the writing you do. Does a well-written memo or report reflect more than your ability to write well? Indeed, well-written correspondence shows more than the ability to write--it reveals a straight thinker, a good organizer, and a person able to make sound judgments. A good piece of writing can serve as your advocate for many months, even years. Likewise, of course, a poorly written piece can reveal a lack of qualities looked for in promotable people. Writing is, then, a serious business. The record is in the files permanently either to recommend your abilities or to embarrass you and present an obstacle to your progress.

What's Your Attitude About Language?

The second key word in writing is ATTITUDE.

At least part of the difficulty in our use of language stems from our becoming desensitized to words. The flood of oral and written verbiage that we live in today has numbed our language sensibilities. The treatment in this text attempts to resensitize the mind to words and to their basic purpose. Too many writers (probably as a result of their training in the schools) think _only_ in terms of getting the writing done, getting it over with. Often we sign our correspondence with a sigh of relief because a burden has been lifted from our shoulders.

This attitude is often revealed at the beginning of courses like this when students are asked to analyze their writing techniques. One student explained it this way:

> Yes, I have a system for getting my correspondence out of the way. Each morning, regardless of the amount of mail in the incoming basket, I get all my replies on tape by 10 a.m. Then I have the rest of the day to work on other things.

Such a writer puts a premium upon "getting it done" as fast as possible, but <u>how</u> it is done seems remote from his mind. He views language as a commodity to be packaged each day and shipped in an envelope to another location. But there is a vast difference between sending verbal messages and packaging commodities. If a writer conducts his correspondence in such a routine fashion, the result will be ill-planned and incomplete communication. And surveys have shown that one poor letter can start a chain reaction, requiring many more exchanges to resolve the confusion.

In an exercise at the end of this chapter you will be asked to put down and assess your attitude toward writing. Your answers to questions like these will be important in beginning this course:

How do you feel about receiving assignments to conduct research and to record the results in written form?

Are you resentful, do you feel victimized if you receive assignments?

Or do you welcome this as a challenge, an opportunity to demonstrate your abilities in analysis, organization, and presentation of data?

Now at this point you may be impatient to get on with the training, but communications courses should be approached in a slow, thoughtful manner. As educational surveys have revealed, many such courses begin too fast, failing to get across the purposes of the instruction. Students should realize why they are pursuing a field of study and how they can benefit from it.

If you also feel that you are being given propaganda (in the good sense of the word) about approaches to writing, you are entirely correct. For, after all, education is a process of manipulation (again in a positive sense) and of drawing out the potential of students. Therefore, remember the two key words--PURPOSE and ATTITUDE. A healthy attitude toward writing considers its dual purpose--to convey clear messages to your reader and to demonstrate your abilities to fellow-workers and supervisors.

What About Speed-Writing?

Another misleading impression about writing practice should be considered. The modern emphasis on time-saving has led students to expect this training to improve writing speed. But the aim should not be writing faster, at least not immediately, and probably not at all. In fact, this training may cause you to take more time to do your writing. This is nothing to worry about, for better accuracy and precision in your writing is a more worthwhile goal than speed--and better writing takes longer to produce. The time your reader will save because of the improved readability of your correspondence will more than compensate for your labor. Later when the techniques learned in the course become a matter of habit, you _may_ be able to write faster.

In this connection it may be helpful to note the great differences in the rates at which we can think, speak and write. Dr. Ralph Nichols in his article "Listening is Good Business" provides some interesting statistics on this. What he has to say may be some comfort to the writer plodding through a revision of a rough draft:

> On the average in America we talk just 100 words a minute when we speak informatively to an audience. How fast do people out front listen? Or, to put it more accurately, how fast do listeners think in words per minute when they listen?
> We do know...that you will never face an audience of any size at all that does not, on the average, think at an easy cruising speed of at least 400 to 500 words a minute. The difference between speech speed and thought speed operates as a tremendous pitfall...

Now Dr. Nichols was comparing speech and thought speeds, but somewhat the same frustration occurs in writing. We, of course, cannot write at a pace anywhere near 100 words per minute, but our thought processes are zipping along at 400-500 words per minute. As a result the writer often becomes impatient with the laborious work of capturing his thoughts on paper. In commenting on their craft many professional writers (for example, Ernest Hemingway and W. Somerset Maugham) reveal that writing is never easy work. Often they say they agonized for hours in getting a single paragraph just right for publication.

A healthy attitude toward your writing, therefore, should be that it _must be_ a slow process, that you should be patient and realize the great difference between thought speed and writing speed.

Let us consider a few more suggestions for the most efficient use of the materials in the course. First, in a writing class no teacher can expect universal agreement from students about what is good writing practice. Part of any good writer's skill comes from individual ideas about word choice and expression. This forms the writer's own style. Second, to some degree each student will take something different from a writing course. Depending on present writing skills, knowledge, and personality, each student will adopt techniques and use them differently from everyone else. And perhaps no one can use all the advice and information given. What is far more important than a slavish following of the rules will be the exchange of opinions among members of the class, the questions and the discussions that will come about from reading the text and doing the exercises. Third, becoming a good writer is an essentially different process from becoming a good key puncher, typist, or machine operator. Writing involves the mental powers in a very different way than does training for manual skills. As Albert R. Kitzhaber, Professor of English, said as Director of the University of Oregon's Curriculum Study Center:

> There can be no quick way to the development of
> a well-stocked mind, disciplined intelligence,
> and discriminating taste and fluency in language.
> The habit of good writing, like the habit of ethical
> conduct, is of slow growth; it is an aspect of a
> person's general intellectual development, and
> cannot be greatly hastened apart from that
> development.

The Time and the Place for Good Writing

The wise writer will try to determine the best time of the day (or night) and the most suitable place to write. Since all of us have somewhat different inner time clocks, we can improve efficiency by choosing the writing time best for us. Are you an "early-riser" or a late "stayer-upper"? Some do their best intellectual work early in the day, others barely wake up until after noon. If thoughts and their expression are easier for you at an early hour or a late one, try to schedule your writing efforts at the ideal time. A quiet place (if possible) and one where you will not be interrupted constantly should be chosen. Especially for preparing longer pieces of writing a period of several hours of concentrated work is much better than coming back to the project several times during the day. If you assign writing to others and subsequently review correspondence, you will get a much better product by allowing your writer sufficient time and by providing him a quiet place.

Steps in the Writing Process

From time to time the text will present some useful lists to remind the writer of fundamentals. These alone will not solve all of your writing problems. They are not meant to be "gimmicks" but may be helpful to you after the formal part of the course is over. Here is one such list:

1. THINK

2. OUTLINE

3. WRITE

4. REVISE

STEP ONE - THINK

It would hardly seem necessary to mention that thought should precede writing. Yet some writers apparently believe that pens and typewriters (or worse, dictating machines) are capable of thought. Otherwise, how could such examples as the following show up in the mail:

... If you don't receive this letter, let us know.

... This sum will be paid to you in a single amount at the time of your death, which we understand is the way you prefer.

"Boners" like these are the products of "thought-less" writing, that is, communication not based upon the thought process. Try this method -- take a blank sheet of paper and jot down points you want to cover in your letter or report. Make no attempt to list these in any special order or even to phrase complete sentences. Place a number in front of each item.

STEP TWO - OUTLINE

Many writers have a prejudice against the term "outline," mainly because the word sounds like work--and indeed it is. But this is the crucial step, for without a logical pattern writing lacks effectiveness. Try this method: Work on your random list of topics from Step One. You will begin to see which numbered items belong with which others in the list. It may help to draw lines connecting the numbers of items belonging together. Now you have begun to outline -- to impose a pattern on your material. Take your time on this outlining phase -- even lay the outline aside for awhile and come back to it later. Don't rush this step, for here the battle for clear writing is won or lost.

<u>Forming the Final Outline</u>: Finally in this step expand your short outline by adding sub-topics. Here is a sample three-level outline:

1. Using plain English
   a. A well-prepared publication has all of its required parts
   b. A publication in plain English should include --
      (1) Effective organization
      (2) Directness in writing
      (3) Logic in writing
      (4) Effective style

2. Measuring grade level

STEP THREE - WRITE

Many writers mistakenly begin at this point, forgetting the two important preliminaries to good writing -- thinking and organizing of thoughts. Now using your outline, write a rough draft as rapidly as you can. This will introduce continuity into your sentences and paragraphs. Don't try to polish the text, substitute words, or improve transitions at this point. These improvements will be brought in with the next step.

STEP FOUR - REVISE

Several more drafts may be necessary, especially on important pieces of writing. Now you may need to write a good introductory and summary paragraph. Read your near-final draft aloud to check for clear transitions and over-all clarity. Set the draft aside for awhile and look at it again before preparing the final copy. This will give you a more objective view of your own work. Finally, let someone else read it to check for smoothness and readability.

If all this sounds too difficult, take comfort from the words of Sinclair Lewis, the American novelist, who was once addressing a college class of writers. After a glowing introduction from the professor of the class, Lewis asked:

> "How many of you would like to learn to write?"
> As all hands raised enthusiastically, Lewis
> replied, "Then go home and write."

Now you have really read the introduction to the text. The word "introduction" was not used as the title because students tend to skip the preliminaries to get on to the more important chapters. Since laying the groundwork is important in a writing course, we will consider some basic principles of communication in the next chapter.

Exercise 1* Chapter One YOUR WRITING INVENTORY

1. Write a paragraph below introducing yourself to the instructor. Include your job title and describe the main duties that you perform in your position.

   _____
   _____
   _____
   _____

2. What kinds of writing do you perform on your job? List them below by types, for example, letters, memos, regulations, reports, messages, performance appraisals, etc.

   _____   _____   _____
   _____   _____   _____
   _____   _____   _____

3. Please classify the types of writing (listed in 2, above) that you do according to their purpose. Then in the second column estimate the percentage of your correspondence for each general purpose:

   Purpose of Writing   Percentage

   To direct

   _____   _____
   _____   _____
   _____   _____

   To inform

   _____   _____
   _____   _____
   _____   _____

   To persuade

   _____   _____
   _____   _____
   _____   _____

*College students should adapt this exercise to analyze the writing required of them in college classes.

Your Writing Inventory--page 2

4. Indicate below the destinations for your correspondence:

   Internal (within your company or organization)   Percentage

      Upward (to your superiors)   _____

      Across (to those on your own level)   _____

      Downward (to those below your level)   _____

   External (outside your company or organization)   _____

5. What is the usual educational level of your readers (college graduate, high-school graduate, or below high school level)?

   _____

6. Write a paragraph below describing the tone most of your writing had during the last week or month. For example, would you term it cold, blunt, humble, tactful, understanding, etc.? After you have chosen some terms to describe your writing, explain why you wrote in this way.

7. Write a paragraph below explaining the methods you are currently using to prepare and accomplish your correspondence. Please include such topics as these: Do you have clearly in mind what you want to say before beginning to write? Do you use a written outline or do you trust your memory? Do you use a dictating machine or dictate to a secretary? Do you write a draft first and then revise it? (Note: Be frank in your responses--they will greatly aid the instructor!)

8. Write a paragraph below, citing what you believe to be the main problems in business, government and academic writing. Your answer could cover your own difficulties or those of other writers, or both.

Exercise 2　　　　　　　Chapter one　　　　A WRITING METHOD

Directions:　Using the THINK-OUTLINE-WRITE-REVISE method suggested in Chapter One, go through the steps to prepare one paragraph of about fifty words on this subject: the reasons you have taken this college or training course and what benefits you hope to gain from it.

THINK　(Jot down ideas just as they occur to you in phrase or fragment form. Try to list more ideas than you will need so that later you can select the best ones.)

a. _____
b. _____
c. _____
d. _____
e. _____
f. _____
g. _____
h. _____
i. _____

OUTLINE　(Arrange the topics from the list above under headings. You may have to think of appropriate main headings--1,2,3, etc.--if they are not found in your list above.)

Note:　Use more headings if you need them.

1. _____
_____
_____
_____
_____

2. _____
_____
_____
_____
_____

3. _____
_____
_____
_____
_____

A Writing Method--2

WRITE		(Prepare a rough draft of your material--write this
		as rapidly as you can.)

REVISE		(Write a final version of your material.)

Exercise 3   Chapter One   ARRANGING AN OUTLINE

Directions: Arrange the following topics in a logical order
              beside the outline symbols below:

              Conclusion, evaluations, and judgments
              Definition of the problem
              Recommendations and proposals for action
              Statement of the problem
              Work done to verify possible solutions
              History of the problem
              Possible solutions to the problem

1.

   a.

   b.

2.

3.

4.

5.

1-13

Chapter One -- Applications

1. Would you believe that these "boners" were actually mailed by thought-less writers?

    a. We have been authorized to make monthly advances to Ms. Wade.

    b. Sid Walters contracted pneumonia, which was brought on by a weekend condition.

    c. He winds up his mouth as Department Head next month.

    d. We can't understand why you resent our inquiring about your bad habits.

    e. Our recent letter to you has been returned to us marked "Deceased." If this is correct, will you please verify it? Then write us what your plans are for paying off the unpaid balance of $20.46. We sincerely hope that everything will go well with you.

2. Here are some inspirational quotations. Read them over from time to time during the course:

    a. "I don't advise you to start talking until you have begun thinking. It's no good opening the tap if there is nothing in the tank." Clarence Randall

    b. "The first executive function is to develop and maintain a system of communication." Chester I. Barnard

    c. "If business has a new motto, 'Communicate or Founder' would seem to be it." Editors of _Fortune_

    d. "Disorganized, illogical writing reflects a disorganized, illogical (and untrained) mind." Anonymous

    e. "Craving for status that has not been earned plays a regrettable part in the current urge to communicate." Clarence Randall

    f. "His reasons are as two grains of wheat hid in a bushel of chaff: you shall search all day ere you find them, and when you do, they are not worth the search." W. Shakespeare

    h. "Reading maketh a full man; conference a ready man; and writing an exact man." Francis Bacon

Questions and/or Comments for Class Discussion

COMMUNICATION THEORY

CHAPTER 2

PART ONE

Chapter Two--Communication Theory

Objectives of Chapter Two:

1. To cite the relationship between communication and performance.

2. To emphasize the connection between the "real world" and the "word world."

3. To explain denotative and connotative values in word usage.

4. To point out how to achieve objectivity in writing.

Communication and Performance

Why is it that communications in industry and government are often more of an obstacle than an aid to the efficiency of the organization? First, it may be that employees are not sufficiently aware of the crucial importance of clear, concise, and effective writing. This course will attempt to bring about that awareness. Secondly, communicators may fail to consider how emotional relationships influence their daily contacts with others. Indeed, an effective message often depends more on "how it is said" than on "what is said." A subtle connotation triggered by an ill-chosen combination of words can seriously affect the communication. No matter how fondly we may wish it, message-giving and receiving are seldom purely rational--for emotion plays an important part.

In addition we often assume that a good accountant, word processor, or engineer will almost automatically be a good communicator. But it often happens that employees with the best professional preparation have had inadequate training in writing and speaking skills. It does little good to have great ideas if we cannot convey them clearly and effectively to others. The course, therefore, will encourage a critical analysis of writing habits, always keeping the reader in mind.

What Price Communication?

The dollar cost of producing letters, memos, and reports continues to rise. Since the "paper chase" is here to stay, communication costs will require an increased share of budgets in government agencies and business firms. But the sheer expense, great as it is, should not be the main concern. Poor writing costs an organization far more in lost customers, inefficiency, and poor decision-making than the money paid for paper and postage. The goal of this course, then, is to train employees to prepare effective messages at their own desks. The better this goal is achieved, the more cost-saving will be realized.

Real World vs Word World

If communication is to be improved and costs reduced, we need to realize just what we are attempting as communicators. The truth is we are trying to turn our impressions of the world around us into words--a clumsy medium at best. As writers we must work with words while other communicators, those using another art form, enjoy a considerable advantage over us. Other artists (the writer is an artist, too) work with physical materials--the painter with paints and brushes, the sculptor with stone, the musician with sounds. But the writer must use an essentially "unreal" and lifeless medium--black marks on paper to represent physically existing things. To overcome this obstacle, writers must wrestle with words which often defy and tantalize them in the attempt to create an adequate record of their thoughts and opinions. Let us address this problem by examining some basic communication theory.

In a sense we all live in three "worlds." First, the "real" world of things, events, and people; these we know through our daily experience. Our knowledge of this real world, of course, is gained through sense impressions and is affected by what we have learned through education and experience. Second, in order to communicate we must translate these impressions we have gained from the real world into words. By means of language, a convenient set of symbols, we convert the real world into a verbal substitute for it. But problems often arise because the real world is dynamic and ever-changing while the word world is static and unchanging. Third, an "idea" world must be created by the words we use, enabling us to reach the minds of others. The following diagram shows the relationships among the three "worlds":

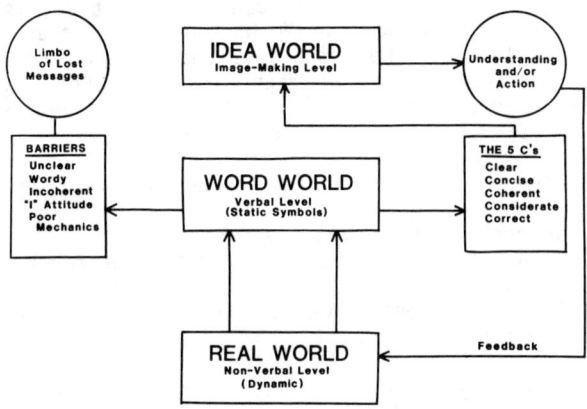

Figure 1

Therefore, realize what you are actually doing as a communicator, either as writer or speaker. You are representing the real world using a set of symbols called words. If you are a skillful writer, you choose the right words and arrange them in the right order. The result should be a readable account of the real world from which it is drawn. But even the best-trained writer can offer no guarantee that his language can present the real world completely to the reader or listener. For example, have you ever wondered why your account of an exciting vacation trip falls flat when you try to tell others about it? Usually you soon note lack of interest in your listeners and end by saying, "Well, you have to go and see it for yourself."

Words in Action, the text title, points up the real function of language: words in themselves may be useless unless they actively serve the writer's purpose (remember this key word from Chapter One?).

Indeed there is no meaning in language itself; there is meaning only as someone reacts to words, spoken or written. The meaning of a word exists in us and in our readers and listeners. A word can mean anything if you and I agree upon it. Justice Holmes once wrote:

> A word is not crystal, transparent and unchanged; it is the skin of a living thought and may vary greatly in color and content according to circumstances and the time in which it is used.

In figure 1 note the labels used for the three levels in the center of the diagram: Non-Verbal Level, Verbal Level, and Image-Making Level. The successful communicator always keeps in mind the goal--to create the right images in the reader's mind. Words make images that either serve the writer's purpose or defeat it.

What kind of image is created by the following sentences?

1. We don't see how you could have failed to understand our clear statement of policy on returning merchandise.

2. As a retail outlet we can't be expected to service claims as small as yours.

Could language like this create anything but irritation, ill-will, and anger? Is this what the writer set out to do? Both sentences feature the "I" attitude--thinking egotistically of one's own interests and ignoring those of the reader. The "you" attitude, on the other hand, teaches the writer to be considerate and to address the reader as one human being to another.

Success in communicating may also be adversely affected by the following all-too-human tendencies:

1. <u>Stereotyping</u>. All of us view the real world through glasses colored by our own background, education, and experience. We try to make the real world neatly fit into what psychologists call our "belief systems," categories we try to impose upon reality. We think too often that if we find a <u>name</u> for people or things or pin a label on them, we have said all there is to say about the subject. But neat classifications often fail to allow for the differences existing in the real world. Consider the injustice and prejudice in statements like these:

    a. If you know one, you know them all. They're all alike--shiftless, lazy, dirty, etc.

    b. No wonder he's in trouble. All the people in that part of town are wild. He never was any good.

    c. Believe me. You'll always have trouble with (fill in any group). Never trust any of them.

Notice the danger of words like <u>all</u>, <u>never</u>, <u>always</u>. They attempt to stereotype people, ignoring the differences. Words like <u>all</u>, <u>never</u>, <u>everybody</u> deny the uniqueness of human beings; they assume the ability to predict human behavior exactly.

2. <u>Narrowing</u>. We, of course, also see the real world in terms of our own occupations and professions. The accountant is likely to perceive an issue somewhat differently from an engineer, a personnel manager differently from a shop foreman, etc. For example, suppose we were to ask a farmer, a geologist, and an artist to view a country scene, then to write an account of what each saw. They all might begin with a general description but would probably continue by concentrating on their special interests--the farmer on the richness of the land for cultivation, the geologist on the contours and rock formations, and the artist on how to reproduce the color and beauty of the scene.

3. <u>Mapping</u>. As a result of stereotyping and narrowing many of us have ready-made "maps" in our heads about people and events. The map may or may not correspond with reality. If it does not, we take from the real world only what fits the map and ignore the rest. Just as false maps will lead us nowhere, the person with such a "closed" mind will be led into false judgments and bad decisions.

Of course, since each of us is a unique individual, our writing is bound to reflect our own backgrounds and interests. But clearer thinking and more logical writing come from an awareness that our conclusions may be based in part upon stereotypes, narrow views of the world, and false maps in our heads.

Another useful practice for the writer involves an understanding and application of the term "the abstraction process" explained in the next section.

The Abstraction Process

Let us again refer to Figure 1. What occurs between the Real World and the Word World levels in the diagram is called "abstracting." The term derives from a Latin word meaning "to draw from." By using our senses we must first draw data from the real world of existing things; then to reach the minds of others we convert this data into words. This, of course, is the crucial step in the communication process--and the reason this textbook exists. Through the data-gathering, outlining, and revision process, writers struggle to find the best words to <u>represent</u>

reality. The following so-called "Ladders of Abstraction" attempt to give graphic form to this concept. Note how increasingly obscure an idea becomes as expression moves to higher verbal levels. (See further treatment of this in Section A of Chapter Three.)

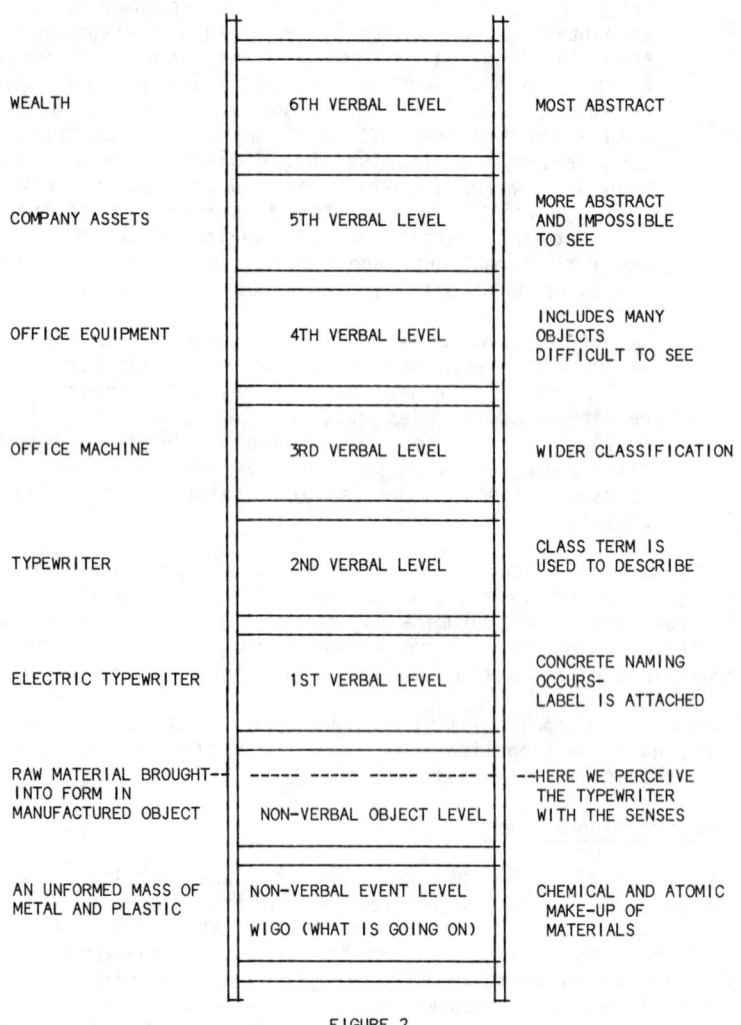

FIGURE 2

Note on the following ladder how emotional inferences made about another person's actions lead to abstract and irrational conclusions. One of the marks of a truly mature person is the ability to think about reality in a rational way--then to be able to use relatively objective, non-emotional language to describe it.

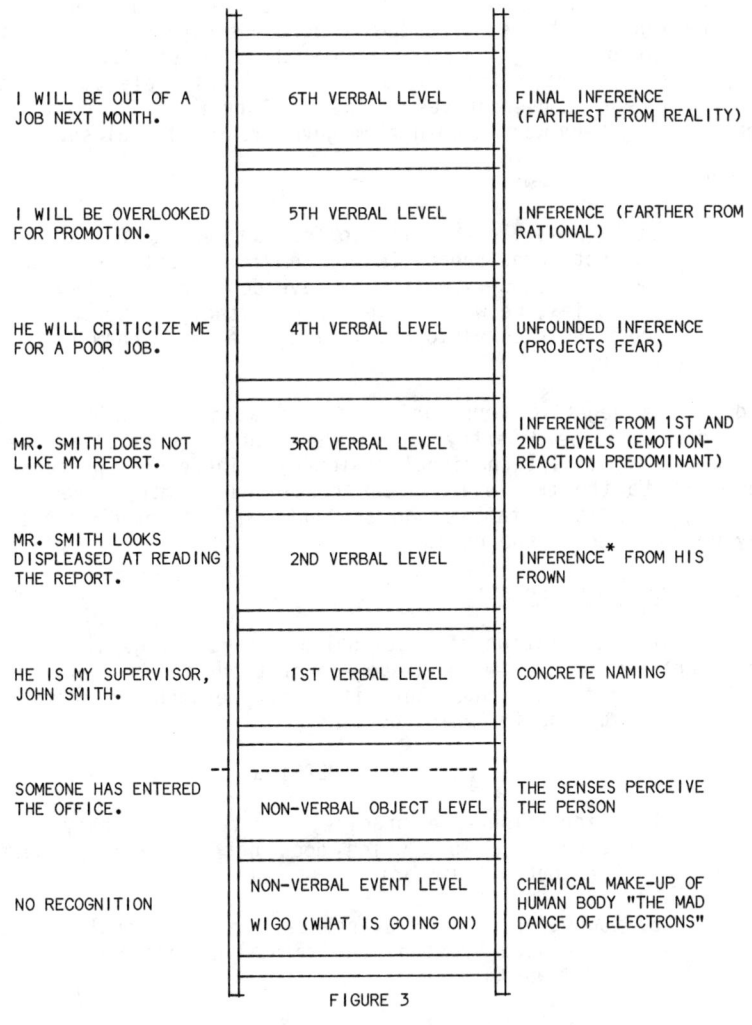

I WILL BE OUT OF A JOB NEXT MONTH.	6TH VERBAL LEVEL	FINAL INFERENCE (FARTHEST FROM REALITY)
I WILL BE OVERLOOKED FOR PROMOTION.	5TH VERBAL LEVEL	INFERENCE (FARTHER FROM RATIONAL)
HE WILL CRITICIZE ME FOR A POOR JOB.	4TH VERBAL LEVEL	UNFOUNDED INFERENCE (PROJECTS FEAR)
MR. SMITH DOES NOT LIKE MY REPORT.	3RD VERBAL LEVEL	INFERENCE FROM 1ST AND 2ND LEVELS (EMOTION-REACTION PREDOMINANT)
MR. SMITH LOOKS DISPLEASED AT READING THE REPORT.	2ND VERBAL LEVEL	INFERENCE* FROM HIS FROWN
HE IS MY SUPERVISOR, JOHN SMITH.	1ST VERBAL LEVEL	CONCRETE NAMING
SOMEONE HAS ENTERED THE OFFICE.	NON-VERBAL OBJECT LEVEL	THE SENSES PERCEIVE THE PERSON
NO RECOGNITION	NON-VERBAL EVENT LEVEL WIGO (WHAT IS GOING ON)	CHEMICAL MAKE-UP OF HUMAN BODY "THE MAD DANCE OF ELECTRONS"

FIGURE 3

* Inferences will be taken up later in the book.

2-7

The following chapters of this text should teach writers how to exert better control over words. Without that control words can take ideas in directions quite contrary to the writer's purposes. In fact, some words take on a life of their own, straying very far from their original meanings. If a writer fails to take this into account, his meaning can miss the mark completely. For example, consider the word <u>detente</u>. Derived from a highly respected French source and meaning "an easing of tension between nations," <u>detente</u> has suddenly become a highly unpopular word in American diplomacy. Unaccountably the word shifted to imply a giving in to Russian demands, a position intolerable to political moderates and conservatives alike. Therefore, a politically embarrassing term was dropped from government officialese.

Or as Senator William Fulbright said:

> It is possible that if Mao Tse-Tung and Ho Chi Minh had not borne the title of 'Communist' but otherwise had done exactly what they have done in their two countries, we would have accepted their victories over their domestic rivals and lived with them in peace.

Indeed the negative connotation of the word "Communist," intensified by the Joe McCarthy era in the 1950's, is still a powerful influence in our international diplomacy. Therefore, writers must be alert to the emotional values contained in many words in our language. If they fail to do so, entirely unwanted impressions may be conveyed to the reader.

<u>Denotation and Connotation</u>

This consideration of emotional meanings brings us to a very important aspect of word usage--denotation and connotation as parts of a word's meaning. The difference between the terms might be clarified by the following outline:

WORD MEANING

1. Denotation--the precise, limited dictionary definition of a word which does not go beyond a limited or controlled meaning.

2. Connotation--the overtones, the emotional attitudes suggested by using the word, the peripheral meanings of a word.

    a.   Personal connotations--these would differ for each one of us. Family or social and professional groups often have their own connotative values for words. These vary too greatly for formal study.

    b.   Common connotations--the attitudes or personal feelings ordinarily expected to accompany the use of a word for almost all educated users of the language.

For example, the word "father" is defined in the dictionary as "male parent relating to me." But this is its bare bones, denotative meaning. As each one of us uses the term "father," especially with the personal adjective before it "my father," the term takes on emotional connotations relating to our own family circle. These meanings, however, would be individual and different for each of us.

Consider, on the other hand, the great difference in meaning between the word "dog" and words such as mongrel, cur, hound. Or, according to a well-known saying, the word "firm" can be declined as follows: I am firm, thou art obstinate, he is pig-headed. The words all have the same objective, denotative meaning, but very different attitudes have been introduced by different choices.

The use of emotionally charged words is not, of course, to be universally condemned. Poetry would be virtually impossible without them; likewise effective prose must bring in connotative values. In Keats' "Eve of St. Agnes," often termed one of the most sensuous poems ever written, these lines occur:

    He followed through a lowly archéd way,
    Brushing the cobwebs with his lofty plume.

But the beauty of this passage would be destroyed by substituting fairly denotative words. Note how the following version is not poetic at all:

    Following through a low and narrow hall,
    He swished the cobwebs with his feathered hat.

In business and government reports the writer should think carefully before using highly connotative terms. Even in persuasive writing it is better to use objective, factual data. This will lead to a more dependable basis for decision-making than emotionally charged or inflated language. While absolute objectivity may be impossible, a report writer should consider his own biases and prejudices and make an honest effort to keep them out of his writing.

Make Your Writing Objective

The following suggestions may help to achieve better objectivity in your writing:

1. Use neutral language as much as possible. Avoid expressions with highly positive or negative connotations. Even in persuasive writing inflated terms designed to "sell" an idea may be misleading. When revising your drafts, check your own viewpoint of the material. Have you allowed your own biases to dictate your word choice? Does your writing represent the "real" world as closely as possible? Reports presenting decisions and recommendations should especially reflect unbiased research. Note in the following sentences that the middle choice of word is the most objective; the others reveal the author's attitude:

   a. The (sound, conservative, reactionary) approach of the speaker affected his argument.
   b. His (discreet, cautious, cowardly) action brought about a great many changes.
   c. He was (transferred, discharged, fired) from his position.
   d. (Solicitude, Concern, Annoyance) marked his reaction to the crisis.
   e. The press conference clearly revealed the position of the (statesman, official, bureaucrat).
   f. His (level-headed, unbiased, fanatical) attitude is obvious.
   g. The group (cooperated, acted, conspired) to bring about the consensus.
   h. The committee (proved, showed, claimed) that the idea was sound.
   i. Let me try to (clarify, explain, apologize for) the possible confusion.
   j. The secretary was (meticulous, careful, fussy) about proper filing procedures.

2. Check your language for factual content. Before preparing your final draft, ask yourself these questions. Have you included all the pertinent data? Is your material _presented_ as fact, but it really consists of inferences and judgments? (Chapter Six will examine these terms fully.) Is your data current and relevant? Have you emphasized the important facts yet covered the less-important ones?

3. Check for possible slanting (language designed for a favorable or an unfavorable presentation of the facts).

   Your presentation of the facts should be in a proper framework to allow the reader to interpret them correctly. For example, the following fails to provide a basis for judgment: "In our survey we found that eighteen of our present accounting staff are in favor of the proposed change." The reader has no way of knowing what percentage of the entire group the number eighteen represents. Rephrase the statement to read: "Our survey revealed that eighteen of the twenty-five accountants favored the change."

   In your reporting you should also try to represent conflicting impressions as fairly as possible. For example, a biased reporter might use one of the following statements without qualifying it: (a) "His briefing was delivered in a halting, seemingly ill-prepared fashion" or (b) "His presentation was greeted at many places by applause from his audience." A fairer, more objective balance might be achieved by combining the two views: "Although his delivery was hesitant, the briefing was interrupted by applause when he covered the following points: etc."

Summary

In this chapter we have approached language as a symbol-system, particularly as an abstraction from reality. The words themselves are not the final goal in the communication process--the meaning they convey is often more important than the precise dictionary definitions. Finally, we have tried to see practical applications for these concepts in business and government writing. The following list of precautions in our use of language may be useful reminders:

1. A word is a _symbol_--the _idea_ behind it is the real goal in the use of language.

2. Words cannot entirely be trusted to represent precisely and accurately what we think or feel.

3. Words sometimes mean different things to different people.

Chapter Two -- Applications

1. Observe in the following two paragraphs how the choice of vocabulary used can slant a paragraph to one emotional extreme or the other. Which would be the more persuasive? Which seems to violate the reasonable and factual bases for writing?

   a. Can we tolerate for another term in office the crooked scoundrel who managed somehow by dirty dealing to get himself elected in the first place. If we rid our political system of this menace, we will at the same time reduce the stupidity and cupidity of the Washington establishment. Such bureaucrats only manage to stay in power by buying the votes of the nonproductive elements in society.

   b. With malice toward none, with charity for all; with firmness in the right as God gives us to see the right, let us strive on to finish the work we are in; to bind up the nation's wounds; to care for him who shall have borne the battle, and for his widow, and his orphan--to do all which may achieve and cherish a just and lasting peace among ourselves, and with all nations. (Abraham Lincoln)

2. After the last lecture in this class or after any other oral presentation, try to recall what thoughts (other than the topics being presented) came to your mind at some time during the session. Probably you will remember quite a few interruptions in your thought process. Did these interfere seriously with your ability to follow the main topics being presented? Does this reveal anything about your listening abilities?

3. Comment on the acceptability of these statements as representations of reality:
   a. Pigs are called pigs because they are such dirty animals.
   b. A snake is called a snake because it is slimy and scaly.
   c. The sun is called the sun because it shines brightly and is in a central position in the solar system.
   d. Stars are called by that name because they appear to have points when we look at them at night.

4. Does the following exchange indicate a truth about language use? Which one?

> An interviewer was questioning a factory worker about his opinion of the "closed shop." The worker replied: "It's a matter of opinion, but myself, I prefer a little ventilation."

5. Examine the following passage in terms of high or low level of abstraction:

> The attached memorandum for record has been reviewed as requested. While the opinion of this office accords with that expressed in the portion of the memorandum styled "Current Status," we prefer to bottom the conclusion reached on the following findings, thereby avoiding a literal adoption of material delineated in the memorandum under the headings "Regulatory Support" and "Reasoning."
>
> a. It is assumed, arguendo, and perforce a paucity of evidence, that the supplies or services covered by the letter contract were required to serve a bona fide need for the coming FY as enunciated by the Comptroller General of the United States.

6. In the following lists of near synonyms select the "core" word, the one with the least connotation. Then write down the connotative values of the other words in each list:

Group One	Group Three
assignment	novel
mission	fresh
program	new
schedule	original
plan	innovative
procedure	new-fangled
practice	unique
policy	different

2-13

Group Two	Group Four
slay	know-how
murder	ingenuity
assassinate	skill
kill	knowledge
slaughter	ability
annihilate	facility
decimate	capability
execute	talent

7. Note the differences in connotation between the following sets of words:

    average   - mediocre   responsibility - blame
    inexpensive   - cheap   fortunate   - lucky
    residence   - house   adventurer   - adventuress
    animal   - beast   secret agent   - spy
    steed   - horse   innovative   - radical

8. Here is a sentence taken from a recent letter written to a large group of educators:

    "We need every available person with concern for and wisdom about this aspect of education if we are to amend the contradiction of an assurance of the availability of an education to those qualified and the denial of that education by the economic factor."

    TRANSLATION (removing deadwood and verbiage):

    "We should make sure that no able student is kept out of college for lack of money."

Questions and/or Comments for Class Discussion

GOOD WRITING IS CLEAR

CHAPTER 3

PART TWO

Chapter Three--Good Writing Is Clear

Objectives of Chapter Three:

1. To stress the readability of clear writing.
2. To emphasize using the simple rather than the complex word or expression.
3. To illustrate jargon in writing and show how to avoid it.
4. To encourage the use of specific and concrete expression rather than general and abstract.

Now that we have examined the general elements in the use of language in Part One, let us examine the more specific virtues of good communication. While we can never have a 100% guarantee of being understood, by earnest effort we can bring the 5 C's into our writing: clear, concise, coherent, considerate, correct. Note that the first and most important "C" is CLEAR. Clarity is crucial to good writing--without it successful message-receiving is impossible. This chapter, therefore, will offer practical advice about how to write clearly.

One of the truths about communication, known by most writers, is that the very act of planning and outlining often serves to clarify thought. Thought processes, as pointed out in Part One are rapid and somewhat chaotic. But thoughts can often be brought under control and disciplined by writing them down in orderly fashion. This statement, from a former President of the American Management Association, stresses the importance of writing it down:

> The firm foundation upon which good communication is built is clarification of thought. Before thought can be transmitted effectively, it must be clear. A poor print can be made from a good negative, but a good print never can be made from a poor negative.
>
> Writing is the most effective means I know for clarifying thought....
>
> If an individual has a sincere, deep yearning to clarify his own thinking, there is no better way to do it than to put it in writing....

A. <u>Use</u> <u>Concrete</u> <u>Terms</u>

To illustrate his point the author of the above quotation used an analogy to photography. In his comparison the thought process is compared to the photographic negative; the piece of writing is the print. The successful writer often makes the new idea clearer by comparing it to a more familiar process. This principle, incidentally, is one of the oldest and soundest methods used in teaching. And the writer must be a good teacher.

Note how the following examples depend for their success upon unusual comparisons:

1. From a technical paper on jet propulsion: The principle of thrust in a jet engine is similar to the action of an inflated toy balloon after you release it in the air. The pressure on the sides of the balloon propel it forward. In the jet engine, etc.

2. From an industrial report: The insulating material failed to meet the test of an increased current load. In approximately five minutes the material charred and burned, creating an acrid odor like that of burned string beans.

Writing becomes more graphic when the action is described in concrete terms. Concrete terms enable us to visualize an idea while abstract terms have no image-making power. For example, the terms <u>freedom</u>, <u>justice</u>, <u>courage</u>, <u>efficiency</u>, <u>cooperation</u> are all abstract. Can you see, feel, or touch any of these? If the idea referred to cannot be understood in terms of the senses, it is abstract. Abstract words stand for thoughts about things. On the other hand, <u>office</u>, <u>Building 60</u>, <u>The Pentagon</u>, <u>room</u>, <u>pencil</u> are concrete words--they refer to physically existing things.

Remember Chapter Two on Communication Theory and the emphasis on reaching the "Image-making" level. Concrete words produce pictures in the reader's mind while too many abstract words present fuzzy ideas.

> PRINCIPLE: While, of course, you cannot avoid using some abstract words, your paragraphs should come down to earth by using concrete references as often as you can.

To make your abstractions concrete try to realize where expressions fit into a diagram like the following:

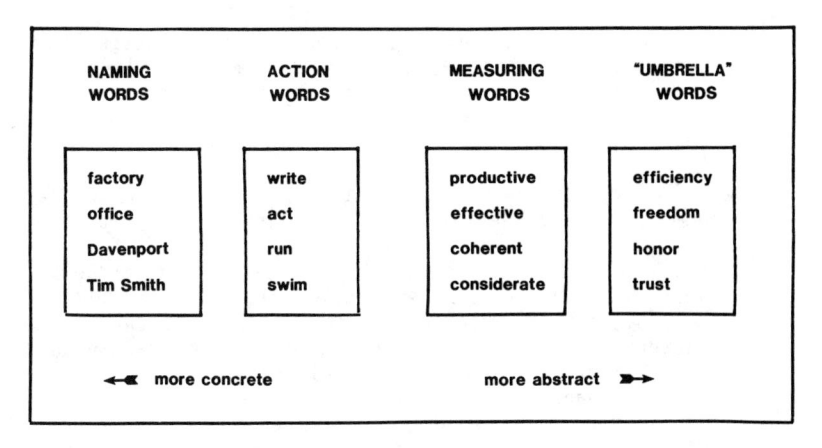

NAMING WORDS	ACTION WORDS	MEASURING WORDS	"UMBRELLA" WORDS
factory	write	productive	efficiency
office	act	effective	freedom
Davenport	run	coherent	honor
Tim Smith	swim	considerate	trust

◄── more concrete   more abstract ──►

FIGURE 4

Handling abstractions often requires breaking the "umbrella" term down into its concrete components. For example, to say "Joe Smith is an efficient employee" may include many of his abilities--communications skill, ability to get along with others, dependability, etc. Joe Smith's abilities, however, would be better described in terms of what he can actually do or has done.

Make your understanding of abstract words more concrete by applying questions like these:

> What special actions or qualities make up this general idea?
> What actions are typical of people or things possessing this quality or force?
> Under what circumstances or in what situations are these actions performed?

Then, if possible, express the idea concretely--the reader will find it much easier to understand you.

A leading cause of dullness or fuzziness in writing is "dead-level abstracting." Dead-level abstracting means to choose expressions like those on the extreme left or extreme right of the table in Figure 4. The secret of good writing is to combine the abstract and the concrete within the same paragraph. In fact (as we will see in the Chapter on Coherence) the pattern for a well-developed paragraph is a topic sentence (usually tends to be abstract) followed by supporting material (the concrete details, examples and facts). Of course, we must use some abstract statements, but these should be illustrated by using concrete and specific data to support them.

The following sentence is difficult to understand because of the high-level abstract terms used:

> Although standard econometric techniques are not satisfactory for estimating a regional econometric policy model, an operational heuristic method can be used for the impact of public works making casual inference of the results upon small economies.

The next example, however, has the opposite fault--it needs rearrangement, placing the abstract idea first in the paragraph:

> But our motive is more than self-interest. We know, because we rub shoulders with people, at work and in the community, that it is important. We realize that a solid background in English is a prerequisite to happiness and well-being. Without a reasonably good command of English --as a means of communication--we are not educated for personal happiness. Even apart from the smooth operation of our jobs, there must be a feeling of personal success in the exciting business of making a living.

B. Use Specific Terms

The reader will also have more trouble handling big bites of information (general terms) than smaller ones (specific terms). In this list notice the ever-widening frame of reference: Shop M, Building 220, a manufacturing installation, a military arsenal, a government facility.

Isn't it much easier to get the picture in Shop M than in a government facility? Of course, the same comment that was made about concrete versus abstract expression applies here--you cannot avoid using some general references, but when you can, reduce them to more specific examples.

Remember the treatment of the "abstraction ladder" in Figure 2 (see Page 2-6). Terms toward the bottom of the ladder are easier to visualize because they are more concrete and specific. Electric typewriter is clearer to any reader than wealth. Or as shown in the chart in Figure 3 (see page 2-7), as you go up the ladder an irrational attitude of insecurity develops to widen the gap between the real and the imagined.

SUGGESTION:

> To assist the writer in finding more concrete and specific word choices, a thesaurus such as Roget's is helpful. A thesaurus or a book of synonyms will suggest many different ways of expressing an idea. The writer can usually select a more concrete and specific phrase from the many listed.

C. Clarify Your Purpose

Chapter One emphasized PURPOSE as the key word for this course. As in most other human activities, if we know our goals in communication, achieving them will become much easier. A useful practice, before you begin to write anything, is to phrase, in a sentence or two, your statement of purpose. For example, notice how each of these statements indicates a different purpose--to persuade, to inform, or to direct:

1. In this memo I am trying <u>to persuade</u> my supervisor to change our inventory method to a new, more efficient system.

2. In this memo I am trying <u>to inform</u> the Project Manager about recent research on packaging techniques.

3. In this report I am trying <u>to direct</u> the reader to follow a series of steps in installing new equipment at Lock and Dam 15.

Figure 5

If you find it difficult to phrase your statement of purpose, consider it a warning. Topics that are fuzzy in the mind of the writer will be fuzzier still in the mind of the reader!

3-5

Stop, look, listen and THINK--wait until you have a clearly written purpose statement. When you have it, you will find such a sentence an excellent check point to recognize the data appropriate for use in your memo or report. Material that does not support this purpose sentence will be rejected as not serving your central purpose.

> PRINCIPLE: If you begin in a clear and well-organized way, you are far more likely to continue in the same manner.

D. Eliminate Jargon

Jargon goes by many names--governmentese, officialese, federalese, gobbledygook, businessese--and should be rooted out of writing. The reason is simple--rather than contributing to the idea content of writing, jargon obscures it.

Many causes contribute to this production of meaningless words and phrases. Most of the trouble can be traced to lack of discipline in writing habits--particularly a failure to decide upon a clear purpose and insufficient attention to the planning phases. Then, too, some writers consider written English as entirely different from the spoken language. With pen in hand they use a stilted, pompous diction--a kind of English never spoken. Writers like these are using language in an attempt to IMpress the reader rather than to EXpress the thought.

A communications consultant was once asked to suggest ways of simplifying the English in a company manual. He came across this "impressive" statement of policy:

> When the regular period for conserving file copies has elapsed, the supervisor will direct his/her employees to follow proper procedures concerning excess file material. This should be promptly accomplished in accordance with the prescribed regulations for proper disposal.

When the consultant later asked a file clerk to explain the policy, she replied, "Oh, that means that we keeps 'em for five years. Then we checks with the super. If he says o.k., we takes 'em to the basement and burns 'em." Her explanation was somewhat ungrammatical but certainly clearer than the "officialese" version.

During the revision process check yourself on this question: "Did I use any word, phrase, or sentence structure primarily to be recognized as highly educated and therefore able to use big words and heavy sentences?" In fact any phrase you were particularly fond of should be regarded with suspicion. It may be just a "cute" phrase you insisted on using regardless of its relevance.

The jargoneer is a type too familiar in business and government today. The immense size of many American firms and the bureaucracy in government has encouraged the use of a "status seeking" jargon for some writers who feel lost in the crowd. This is not, of course, a new phenomenon. From the earliest times a favorite device for achieving status has been the use of impressive language. Words rightly used can recommend the writer as a superior thinker, but inflated, meaningless jargon can indicate a fuzziness in the writer's mind.

One of the best ways to detect jargon is to ask yourself: "Is this sentence a type of English that would _never_ be spoken?" If so, there are likely to be elements of jargon in the expression. For example, if someone asked you to borrow a pencil, would you hand it over with this remark: "I hand you herewith said pencil, as you recently requested?" Probably you would _say_: "Here's the pencil you wanted, Joe."

Can you recognize the jargon in this example:

> A portion of the unliquidated obligations is
> a result of deliveries effected prior to the
> transfer of the program to headquarters.
> Consequently, an upward adjustment in deliveries
> is necessary for an ultimate reconciliation.

Imagine how this message would be delivered over the phone-- would gobbledygook like this be used? You might say it this way: "Your agency must speed up deliveries during August. This will bring our next year's budget figures into proper balance."

A news item from Washington headed, "Did Simple English Cost Employee His Job?" records one government writer's sad experience:

> Well, it probably was bound to happen. A federal
> employee has charged he was fired because he didn't
> use government gobbledygook in his official reports.
>
> In a suit filed in U.S. District Court...Attorney
> Donald Dalton said his client was fired because he
> dared to write reports in clear, simple English...
>
> The employee had written in one of his reports:
> "The purpose of this order is to formalize
> procedures, policies, authority, and responsibility
> for conducting surveillance of contract."

The FAA sharply criticized the language, apparently because it was too understandable, and instead instructed that it should be written this way: "The purpose of this order is to establish procedures and policies and to determine the authority and responsibility of authoritative personnel for conducting the surveillance contract."

E. <u>Does Shortness Guarantee Clarity?</u>

Conciseness is indeed an important quality of good writing. But clarity should be the primary aim. Many textbooks on improving writing feature conciseness as the answer to all the writer's problems. A short sentence can, however, garble a message.

Here are two examples:

1. It was, nevertheless, attended by substantial definitional complexity and conceptual ambiguity. (11 words)

2. In our early thinking on these issues, we assumed a relatively fixed set of competencies, ranging from the narrowly professional to broader, personality-oriented variables, such as adaptiveness, change orientation, cosmopolitanism, and the like--all these engaged in a determinable organizational environment and a determinate set of tasks. (49 words)

   <u>Analysis</u>: Even though one statement is short and the other lengthy, both are difficult to understand and full of jargon.

   PRINCIPLE: A short sentence can be just as unreadable as a long one. Check first for basic clarity, then for conciseness.

F. <u>Use of "Fad" Words (Neologisms)</u>

What principle should a writer follow in deciding upon word choices? Are newly minted words (neologisms) acceptable in letters, memos, and reports? No simple or easy answers can be given, except to consider the following principle. If your reader considers a word too "cute," strained, or colloquial, you have lost at least a minor skirmish in the battle for clear writing.

But how can you anticipate the reader's reaction to a particular word usage? Again no rigid answers are possible because usage has no fixed boundaries or rules.

Consider the following sentences. Would you risk using any of these, especially if your reader is unknown to you?

. . . My supervisor has really been hassling me about that report.

. . . He really turned out to be a word freak after taking the Effective Writing course.

. . . The briefing was well prepared but the mike kept going on the blink.

A further problem with new usages occurs in the exaggeration implied in words like fantastic and mind-boggling. What does it take anyway to "boggle" a mind? Are there inflated values in expressions like marathon talks, sprawling metropolises, and productive exchanges? Would a reader get a clear meaning from these terms?

New words enter the language more rapidly during eras of great change. New ideas, methods, and social movements bring in hosts of new words to fill new needs. But how many survive? Consider the following examples and what has happened to them:

1. Watergate brought us game plan, stonewall, deep six and launder (under Nixon launder became a dirty word).

2. The drug culture used old words in new ways: bag, grass, scene, pad, narc, vibes, downers and uppers, bummer, trip, and crash.

3. Vietnam gave new meaning to escalate, pacify, and incursion.

Of course some neologisms achieve respectability and do become accepted as part of the language. For example, motel (compound of motor and hotel) and brunch (combines breakfast and lunch) are here to stay. But many neologisms are merely "fad words" and pass quickly from the language. Therefore, because they are unstable, newly coined words should be avoided or used with caution.

Neologisms further show a disturbing tendency to become clichés. Here is a list of a few we have thoroughly exhausted through overuse:

3-9

Hopefully (one of the worst)
The "ize" group--prioritize, definitize, jumboize
The "wise" group--weatherwise, accountingwise, mediawise
From education--parameters, peer groups, evaluation, siblings
From business--upfront, the bottom line, the nitty-gritty, early on, on-going
From computer people--inputs, outputs, printouts, interfaces

As a final example of an annoying and clichéd habit that has swept the country, consider this question: Why do so many speakers hold up two fingers on each hand and wiggle them to indicate "quotes"?

G. Readability Formulas

A number of useful formulas can be used as yardsticks to measure an important aspect of clarity--readability. Of course, the important consideration is "readable for whom?" Highly technical or scientific terms cause no trouble for the reader with background and training in the subject being discussed. But the reader lacking the ability to handle these terms may find them difficult or impossible to understand. When writing is being prepared for multiple readers, for those of varying educational levels, or for readers unknown to the writer, the readability level is especially important.

One of the easiest readability formulas to apply is Robert Gunning's Fog Index, presented in his excellent book, The Technique of Clear Writing.

According to Gunning a writer should follow these simple steps to find the Fog Index of his written material:

1. Figure the average sentence length by dividing the number of words by the number of sentences. Use a sample of 100 or more words in figuring average sentence length. Sentences that have two independent clauses separated by a semicolon are counted as two sentences.

2. Compute the percent of hard words. To do this, count the number of words of three or more syllables in the sample, and divide this number by the total number of words in the sample. Omit the following from the count of hard words:

a. Verbs that are made three syllables by adding "ed" or "es," like "donated," "indorses," "created," or "trespasses."
   b. Combinations of short easy words, like "stockholder," "airliner," "bookkeeper," or "manpower."
   c. Words that are capitalized.
3. Add the average sentence length and the percent of hard words, and multiply by .4. The result is the Fog Index of the material. For example, the Fog Index computation for a 150-word letter containing 10 sentences and 15 words of three or more syllables is as follows:

```
Average sentence length (150 - 10)  = 15
Percent hard words (15 - 150)       = + 10%
                                      ----
                                       25
Fog Index factor                      x .4
Fox Index                             ----
                                       10
```

The formula is based upon only two factors--word choice and sentence length. The assumption is that the longer the words and the sentences, the foggier the meaning. The figure obtained by applying the yardstick represents the years of schooling the reader should have to understand the writing with ease. The average high school graduate can read, with ease, material with a Fog Index of 12 or less. Writing with a Fog Index of more than 12 is in the danger zone and may be hard for the general reader.

For highly technical or scientific writing the Fog Index has limited usefulness. All readers, however, from the graduate engineer to the shop worker, will appreciate the shorter sentences and simpler vocabulary encouraged by this formula.

Other readability formulas suggest keeping the number of words of two or more syllables under 25 percent and the average length of sentences from 17 to 21 words. Another useful technique (to be presented in Chapter Four on conciseness) is to reduce the number of dependent clauses in your writing. Also reducing the number of words of Latin origin in a passage can improve readability. Consider, for example, the Latin sources of the word "transportation":

LATIN:	trans	port	ation
ENGLISH:	across	to carry	the act of

Thus "transportation" conveniently combines into one word the three ideas expressed in the phrase "the act of carrying across."

But note in the following paragraph that the underlined "Latinized" words interfere with the readability:

The <u>production</u> <u>of</u> <u>communications</u> within our <u>organization</u> <u>continues</u> to <u>represent</u> an ever-growing <u>portion</u> of our over-all <u>expenditures</u>. Therefore, we <u>encourage</u> all <u>personnel</u> to <u>conduct</u> an <u>investigation</u> of their own <u>communications</u> <u>practices</u> and, in this way, to <u>attempt</u> to <u>effect</u> a <u>reduction</u> in <u>operating</u> <u>expenses</u>.

PRINCIPLE: Mechanical counting formulas are helpful, but none will <u>insure</u> good readability. Writers are best advised to check their writing using the 5 C's.

H. <u>A Final Test for Clarity</u>

One check on the clarity of your writing may be more valuable than all the previous tips. Read your report aloud! Were there places where it sounded rough, where it was difficult to read with smoothness, or where you ran out of breath before the end of a sentence? If it is to be easily understood, you should be able to read it without effort. A tape recorder can be useful to check the clarity. Record your writing; then sit back and listen--the awkward phrasing will mark the places needing revision. An even better practice is to allow a few days between recording and listening to the playback. By this time you will be more objective in criticizing your own writing.

A few years ago the Bureau of Naval Weapons issued a statement addressed to writers in the agency. No better advice on clarity could be offered:

Our biggest problem in communications is that you're there and we're here! We'd have no problem if we could all get together and talk whenever we wanted to. But we can't do that so we have to resort to writing to "talk" to each other.

At best, writing is a poor substitute for talking. But the closer our writing comes to conversation, the better our exchange of ideas will be. And when you think how 99% of the Bureau's business is conducted by the written word, you realize how important it is to write as simply, clearly and directly as you can. We have a job to do, and we have an obligation to be intelligible to each other.

Clear writing doesn't just happen; it takes practice to say exactly what you mean in the fewest possible words. But you owe it to your readers to make the effort.

A Transition

Now for an illustration of a technique we will take up in detail in Chapter Five on Coherence. The paragraph you are about to read is a look backward as well as forward. It is known as a TRANSITIONAL PARAGRAPH. (The transitional paragraph is both a sub-summary and a preview of material to come.)

We have covered some aspects of CLARITY--the all-important virtue of successful writing--now we will consider the other four C's of good writing: CONCISE, COHERENT, CONSIDERATE, and CORRECT.

Exercise 1   Chapter Three   CLARITY

Directions: Reduce the fog in the following paragraphs by
              writing a clearer version of each. Add concrete and
              specific details where needed, even if you have to
              make them up:

1. In order to make a determination as to reasonableness of price as required by Procurement Procedures and to ensure competitive procurement, it is requested that information be furnished to this installation by the date listed below as to prices paid for similar equipment if you have purchased any of the items listed in paragraph 1.

2. Inasmuch as the undelivered portion of said item to date is deemed by the undersigned to constitute an unconsequential quantity it is determined by this Agency that it would be in the best interest of the Government and the said contractor to consider at this point the contract to be complete with the subsequent delivery of the aforementioned quantity of 58 Hand Taps.

Exercise 1--page two

3. If any drawings depicting a part have been redrawn and the original drawing number used on the new drawing, it is requested that the new drawing numbers be assigned to the redrawn drawings. Further, if in the future a drawing is redrawn, then a new drawing number is to be assigned to the new drawing.

4. On planning your presentation for the review, it is suggested in addition to presenting the normal functions of Quality Assurance, such as methods and techniques utilized in the preparation of the Quality Assurance Provisions and SQUAP's the design of final inspection and test equipment and the demonstrated application and use of these acceptance inspection criteria, consideration be given to stressing the role of the Arsenal as a pilot producer wherein the Quality Assurance element assists in assessing and evaluating the adequacy and accuracy of the technical data package prior to release to industry for competitive procurement.

5. It is the responsibility of each and every manager to properly make arrangements for his particular organization in such a manner compliable with efficient operation, that each employee, regardless of classification, and including himself, will receive the full vacation to which he is duly and contractually entitled.

Exercise 2   Chapter Three   CLARITY

Directions: Rewrite each of the following statements to make
              them more vivid and concrete. You will have to
              invent concrete illustrations.

              Example: To his abstinence from chronic alcoholic
                        indulgence must be attributed his changed
                        condition.
              Revision: He got better because he stopped drinking
                        whiskey every day.

1. The national government emphasized that labor and management must settle their differences.

2. Advancement in industry positions is often dependent upon personal contacts.

3. Last year I took a training course sponsored by the federal government which broadened my mental abilities.

4. One large Midwestern military installation tries to assist its employee's general advancement and improvement.

5. The officer of the law advised us that the area was one of high crime rates and that precautions should be taken when leaving any personal possessions there!

Exercise 2--page two

6. Call the maintenance staff to evaluate the general conditions affecting illumination in the office area.

7. My overall relationship with my supervisor often involves exchange of opinion.

8. The fluctuations in demand for construction and weather conditions often make the salary rates in the building trades highly erratic.

9. Members of our law-making bodies sometimes allow selfish considerations to affect their decisions rather than their basic duty to represent the majority views of their constituents.

10. During their leisure hours the members of the military group tended to indulge in sources of amusement offered in a near-by city.

Exercise 3   Chapter Three   CLARITY

Directions: The following paragraph is an example of writing to
            IMPRESS rather than to EXPRESS. Rewrite the paragraph
            reducing the needlessly difficult terms to simpler
            wording.

1. An investigation is being expeditiously performed on the submitted inadvertency in your reported remuneration for the two-
   week period 30 June to 14 July. Due to the fact that it is
   difficult to ascertain the basic and fundamental reasons
   contributing to the causes of the error, further action at
   this time is precluded; and the matter is held in abeyance.
   Pursuant to the finalizing of the investigation and the submission of requisite data the matter will be expedited. To
   facilitate termination of this case furnish verification from
   your immediate supervisor of aggregate job hours performed
   along with any lost from your incapacitation but which is in
   excess of earned sick-leave allowance. The utilization of
   this data will be the optimum method of consummating this
   matter. Procurement and submission of this information must
   be accomplished by 1 August.

2. Do you think that the following memo is clear? If not,
   rewrite it to clarify the message:

   SUBJECT: Inventory

   Please delete the following items from DRSAR-CPF-F Inventory
   and ADD to DRSAR-CPF-R:

       Three Desks, One Secretary, Two Regular
       Three Wastebaskets
       Three Chairs, Two Secretarial, w/o Arms,
          Rotary, One With Arms, Rotary.
       Three Calculators:
          Monroe   J514203
          Addo   4380049
          Victor   5740944

Exercise 4   Chapter Three   CLARITY

Directions: Judge the following underlined usages as acceptable or questionable in addressing a general reader:

1. The politician showed great <u>charisma</u> in the negotiations with the Soviets.

2. The briefing was really <u>out of sight</u> considering our real needs here.

3. Last year he was <u>into computers</u>; now it seems he's <u>into politics</u>.

4. Too bad they are <u>hung up on environmental</u> issues.

5. He was all right until he became a <u>gambling freak</u>.

6. Salesmen have to be aware of <u>usership</u> to plan sales promotions.

7. We'll have to <u>regularize</u> our personnel policies.

8. The problem was with the <u>fast-breeder</u> reactor.

9. Our goals have to be <u>prioritized</u>.

10. The judge announced that he would hear the <u>palimony suit</u> next week.

Chapter Three -- Applications

1. Is the lack of clarity serious in the following statements?

    a. Since you left, his progress has improved.
    b. You can't have too much education in industry and government today.
    c. I could not fail to disagree with you less.
    d. Please send us the number of your employees broken down by sex.

2. Can you figure out the popular saying referred to in these pompous versions?

    a. A mass of earthy material perennially rotating on its axis will not accumulate an accretion of bryophytic vegetation.
    b. That prudent avis which matutinally deserts the coziness of its abode will ensnare a vermiculate creature.
    c. Certain individuals who are constrained to be domiciled in vitreous structures of patent frangibility should, on no account, employ petrous formations as projectiles.
    d. Aberration is the hallmark of homo sapiens. While condonation and placability are the indica of supermundane omniscience.
    e. It is to be regretted that this speaker lacks a multiplicity of lives which, under prevailing circumstances, might be offered on behalf of his nation.
    f. An ultimate end to corporeal existence is preferred to continued viability without the attendant liberties generally associated with the rights and privileges of a free people.
    g. Hear Ye! This is classified information on a need-to-know basis. British, redcoated, armed, are proceeding in this direction.
    h. The full combat potentials available to me have not been effectuated at this point in time.
    i. Defensive fire operations will commence only after it is possible to discern the distal corneas, surrounding the pupils, of the advancing enemy.
    j. At some unspecified point in time, this speaker assures his certain reversion to this place.

3. Examine these quotations for use of specific and concrete language to achieve effectiveness. Many famous quotations are memorable because of their "image-making" power:

a. Let the word go forth from this time and place, to friend and foe alike, that the torch has been passed to a new generation of Americans--born in this century, tempered by war, disciplined by a hard and bitter peace, proud of our ancient heritage.... (John F. Kennedy)
b. It is with words as with sunbeams--the more they are condensed, the deeper they burn. (Robert Southey)
c. Man is the only creature who blushes, or needs to. (Mark Twain)
d. My foreign aid program will mainly consist of sending money and food to needy people in foreign lands--like Mississippi and Alabama. (Dick Gregory)
e. Except ye utter by the tongue words easy to understand, how shall it be known what is spoken? For ye shall speak into the air. (I Corinthians 14:9)
f. What do you mean "Nothing is ever right"? Even a clock that isn't running is right twice a day. (anonymous)
g. True ease in writing comes from art, not chance,
As those move easiest who have learned to dance.
(Alexander Pope)
h. There is first the literature of knowledge, and secondly the literature of power. The function of the first is to teach; the function of the second is to move: the first is a rudder; the second an oar or a sail.
(Thomas De Quincey)
i. The difference between the right word and the almost-right word is like the difference between lightning and the lightning bug. (Mark Twain)
j. Their style is clear, masculine, and smooth, but not florid; for they avoid nothing more than multiplying unnecessary words or using various expressions.
(Jonathan Swift)
k. But true expression, like the unchanging sun,
Clears and improves whate'er it shines upon,
It gilds all objects, but it alters none.
(Alexander Pope)
l. Poetry is the record of the best and happiest moments of the happiest and best minds.... It is as it were the interpenetration of a diviner nature through our own; but its footsteps are like those of a wind over the sea, which coming calm erases, and whose traces remain only, as on the wrinkled sand which paves it. (Percy Shelley)
m. The world is charged with the grandeur of God.
It will flame out, like shining from shook foil;
(G. M. Hopkins)
n. I should have been a pair of ragged claws,
Scuttling across the floors of silent seas.
(T. S. Eliot)

4. The following "Standard Progress Report: is an invention of William Cohen, China Lake, California. It makes sport of the fact that clichés are often used to cover up lack of information. You will meet many old friends, such as: The considerable difficulty, the unnecessary duplication, the immediate vicinity, and the satisfactory rate.

   Standard Progress Report for Those
   with No Progress to Report

   During the report period which ends--(fill in appropriate date) considerable progress has been made in the preliminary work directed toward the establishment of initial activities. (We are getting ready to start, but we haven't done anything yet.) The background information has been surveyed and the functional structure of the component parts of the cognizant organization has been clarified. (We looked at the assignment and decided that George would do it).

   Considerable difficulty has been encountered in the selection of optimum materials and experimental methods, but this problem is being attacked vigorously and we expect that the development phase will proceed at a satisfactory rate. (George is looking through the handbook.) In order to prevent unnecessary duplication of previous efforts in the same field, it was necessary to establish a survey team which has conducted a rather extensive tour through various facilities in the immediate vicinity of manufacturers. (George and Henry had a nice time in New York.)

   The Steering Committee held its regular meeting and considered rather important policy matters pertaining to the over-all organizational levels of the line and staff responsibilities that devolve on the personnel associated with the specific assignments resulting from the broad functional specifications. (Untranslatable--sorry.) It is believed that the rate of progress will continue to accelerate as necessary personnel are recruited to fill vacant billets. (We'll get some work done as soon as we find someone who knows something.)

5. Try to follow the thought processes of the jargon expert in the following article:

INPUT to OUTPUT, 35 min.

INPUT to OUTPUT, 35 min.

For government employees and bureaucrats who have problems with standard recipes, here's one that should make the grade--a classic version of the chocolate-chip cookie translated for easy reading:

TOTAL LEAD TIME: 35 MIN.
Inputs:
1 cup packed brown sugar
1/2 cup granulated sugar
1/2 cup softened butter
1/2 cup shortening
2 eggs
1 1/2 teaspoons vanilla
2 1/2 cups all-purpose flour
1 teaspoon baking soda
1/2 teaspoon salt
12-ounce package semi-sweet chocolate pieces
1 cup chopped walnuts or pecans

Guidance:

After procurement actions, de-containerize inputs. Perform measurement tasks on a case-by-case basis. In a mixing-type bowl, impact heavily on brown sugar, granulated sugar, softened butter and shortening. Coordinate the interface of eggs and vanilla, avoiding an overrun scenario to the best of your skills and abilities.

At this point in time, leverage flour, baking soda and salt into a bowl and aggregate. Equalize with prior mixture and develop intense and continuous liaison among inputs until well-coordinated. Associate key chocolate and nut subsystems and execute stirring operations.

Within this time frame, take action to prepare the heating environment for throughput by manually setting the oven baking unit by hand to a temperature of 375 degrees Fahrenheit (190 Celsius). Drop mixture in an ongoing fashion from a teaspoon, implement onto an ungreased cookie sheet at intervals sufficient enough apart to permit total and permanent separation of throughputs to the maximum extent practicable under operating conditions.

Position cookie sheet in a bake situation and surveil for 8 to 10 minutes or until cooking action terminates. Initiate coordination of outputs within the cooling rack function. Containerize, wrap in red tape and disseminate to authorized staff personnel on a timely and expeditious basis.

Output:
Six dozen official government chocolate-chip cookie units.

3-23

Questions and/or Comments for Class Discussion

GOOD WRITING IS CONCISE

CHAPTER 4

PART TWO

Chapter Four--Good Writing Is Concise

Objectives of Chapter Four:

1. To present practical revision methods for lengthy sentences.
2. To encourage the use of short words.
3. To point out the strength of "working" verbs.
4. To examine redundant expression, euphemisms, inflated language, and clichés.

Alexander Pope in the Eighteenth Century wrote a warning about verbiage in the following couplet:

> Words are like leaves and where they most abound,
> Much fruit of sense beneath is rarely found.

Writers could hardly find better advice about conciseness than this.

Section E in Chapter Three warned the writer against depending on conciseness alone to guarantee clarity. Mere word-counting will not solve all writing problems. In fact, with planning a skillful writer can construct good long sentences--those exceeding the often-cited limit of 17 to 21 words. The 17-21 figure should be considered not an absolute but an _average_ length. The Fog Index Formula in Step 1 (see page 3-10) allows for sentences of varying length in arriving at an average. But readers do have a toleration point. The following sentence undoubtedly exceeds it:

> Although the inspector was firm in his belief that the design of the protective shield on the equipment would not affect the mechanical performance of the vehicle, it cannot be overlooked that it may well be instrumental in causing problems that may eventuate in affecting its maneuverability in the field. (50 words)
>
> COMMENT: The enormous length here would certainly tax the understanding and the patience of any reader. But the sentence has more serious faults, resulting from failure to plan the sentence and to revise the first draft. Also note the excessive number of dependent clauses--those beginning with "although" and "that." Five separate ideas clutter up the sentence, making it difficult to recognize the main message.

Try This Revision Method:

1. Recognize the main ideas to be conveyed and jot them down as follows:
   a. design does not affect mechanical performance
   BUT
   b. possible problem of maneuverability should be checked

2. Now build two sentences to reflect these main ideas and shorten the phrasing as follows:

The inspector firmly believes that the protective shield design will not affect the vehicle's mechanical performance. Further tests, however, are needed to check the effect on maneuverability. (27 words)

COMMENT: Note that 23 words have been dropped from the original 50-word sentence. Phrasing the main ideas in separate sentences will almost invariably eliminate excess words.

A. Reduce Verbiage

Reducing "verbiage" identifies the non-contributing words in a sentence and eliminates them. Some writers apparently believe that "the more words used the better the message." But excess wording more often obscures than clarifies. Since verbiage bogs down the sentence in a jungle of overlapping structures, a second reading is often required. Even then the poor structure stands in the way of clear comprehension.

Is there any excuse for a statement like this getting on paper?

As you are probably well aware at this particular time, we have just recently been given approval of the specifications prepared by your office outlining engineering details for the installation to be built, and I am sure you can appreciate the difficulties involved at this early date in attempting to determine a more accurate delivery schedule than the one which we originally quoted you.

Such writing comes from an undisciplined mind, apparently more interested in multiplying words than in communication. Try the suggested revision method on the example above:

1. Isolate the main ideas:
   a. specifications have been approved
   b. unable to give a specific delivery date

2. Frame sentences to express these ideas:

   Your specifications have been given final approval for the engineering on the project. We cannot give a specific delivery date now but will do so as soon as possible.

   Note: The revision uses <u>two</u> sentences to express the <u>two</u> main ideas.

B. <u>Use Short Words</u>

Gardner Cowles, the publisher, kept these suggestions framed on his desk:

> Never fear big words.
> Big words name little things.
> All big things have little names--
> Such as life and death, peace and war--
> Or dawn, day, night, hope, love, home.
> Learn to use little words in a big way.
> It is hard to do.
> But they say what you mean.
> When you don't know what you mean--
> Use big words.
> They often fool little people.

Remember the principle from Chapter Three on clarity--make your sentences clear first then make them short. Conciseness does not always provide clarity. One survey taker discovered this when he shortened his question: "How long have you lived at your present address?" to simply: "Length of residence." One reply came back "27 feet, six inches." Or when an overly concise teletype message asked: "How old Gloria Swanson?" The reply came back: Old Gloria fine. How you?" Conciseness should be used only in the service of clarity.

Often the more sophisticated and complex a society becomes the more its members move toward important sounding language. But if we use words for status-seeking reasons, the clarity will suffer! The big word is chosen over the little one--not to EXpress the thought but to IMpress the reader. Our culture has taken on airs--and we tend to substitute our basic Anglo-Saxon vocabulary with impressive sounding words of Latin, Greek, or French origin. Consider the difference in readability between the following sets of words:

Impressive Word	Simple Word
remuneration	pay, salary
domicile	home
held in abeyance	wait, postpone, delay
ameliorate	improve
consummate	complete, end, conclude
facilitate	bring about, make easy
finalize	conclude, end
incapacitated	unable to work, ill, confined
initiate	begin, start
terminate	end, conclude
participate in	take part, join
commitment	promise, agreement
optimum	best, ideal
utilization	use
verification	proof
commence	begin

Words chosen from the left-hand column usually identify a writer trying to bring stature to simple ideas by using an impressive vocabulary. Note how the following example of pompous writing lacks both clarity and conciseness:

> As conditions ameliorate toward the finalizing of the commitment, unless the project is terminated before its expected consummation date, optimum utilization of the facilities should finalize in a successful termination.

> PRINCIPLE: Ask yourself whether your choice of word makes the idea clearer to the reader or is merely an "impressive" word.

C. Use "Working" Verbs

The verb (the action word) carries the power in a sentence. Words can be saved and strength gained by watching your choice of verb. Too often, however, writing takes this form:

> The conclusions to be made from this thorough study are in the direction of leading us at the present time to consider seriously the adoption of the incentive plan. If we were to plan for a full presentation of the pertinent facts for the consideration of employee groups, our judgment is that their opinion would be favorable for adoption.

ANALYSIS: Note that there are no strong verbs in this passage. The writer has smothered the action by using weak linking verbs like <u>are</u>, <u>were</u>, and <u>would be</u>. Note also how "ion" words clutter up the paragraph: <u>conclusion</u>, <u>direction</u>, <u>adoption</u>, <u>presentation</u>, <u>consideration</u>, and <u>opinion</u>. If your writing is heavily burdened with nouns, the verbs will usually be weak connectives.

REVISION: (<u>using working verbs</u>): I believe we should accept the incentive plan. If we present it clearly to our employees, they will favor it.

In the following famous passage from <u>The American Crisis</u> by Tom Paine notice how the verbs carry the message effectively:

These are the times that try men's souls. The summer soldier and the sunshine patriot will, in this crisis, shrink from service of his country; but he that stands it now, deserves the love and thanks of man and woman. Tyranny, like hell, is not easily conquered; yet we have this consolation with us, that the harder the conflict the more glorious the triumph. What we obtain too cheap, we esteem too lightly--'Tis dearness only that gives everything its value. Heaven knows how to put a proper price upon its goods; and it would be strange indeed, if so celestial an article as freedom should not be highly rated.

Make the action part of your sentence do the work--you will express a more precise meaning in a shorter way. In the following list notice how the "little" verb forms like <u>make</u>, <u>take</u>, <u>give</u>, <u>come</u>, etc. are often followed by nouns ending in "ion":

<u>Wordy Phrase</u>   "Working" <u>Verb</u>

give consideration to .... consider
make an investigation .... investigate
take into consideration .... consider
may result in damage to .... damage
come to a decision .... decide
seems to indicate .... indicates
make an adjustment .... adjust
leave out of consideration ..... disregard

PRINCIPLE: Write short, direct sentences by making "working" verbs carry the action.

D. <u>Break</u> <u>Down</u> <u>Elements</u> to <u>Simpler</u> <u>Forms</u>

Voltaire, the French writer, once remarked at the end of a ten-page letter: "I am sorry to have written you such a long letter, but I didn't have time to write you a shorter one." His frank confession reveals a great truth about the revision process--it does take time to produce good writing, but your reader will thank you for it.

A helpful method to cut down verbiage is similar to the function in mathematics of reducing fractions to a common denominator (that is, a smaller number). Try to reduce expression to the simplest (and shortest) grammatical form. Here is a sketchy table illustrating the principal sentence structures (examples of each are underlined):

    Main Clauses
        Example: <u>Writing</u> <u>should</u> <u>be</u> <u>effective</u>, and <u>it</u> <u>should</u> <u>be</u> <u>concise</u>.

    Dependent Clause
        Example: Writing <u>which</u> <u>is</u> <u>concise</u> is effective.

    Verbal Phrase
        Example: Writing, <u>to</u> <u>be</u> <u>effective</u>, is concise.

    Prepositional Phrase
        Example: Writing <u>for</u> <u>effective</u> <u>purpose</u> is concise.

    Word
        Example: <u>Effective</u> writing is concise.

Now, while there may be slight differences in meaning among the various choices, the basic message is the same.

    PRINCIPLE: Why use heavy clause constructions when you could save words by using shorter, simpler structures?

The most frequent offender in the list above is the dependent clause--the one beginning with <u>who</u>, <u>which</u>, <u>that</u>, <u>when</u>, <u>where</u>, <u>although</u>, <u>since</u>, etc. One communications consultant advised her clients to conduct "which" hunts through their first drafts. She singled out the "which" or "that" clause as a source of much wordiness.

The verbiage in the following sentences comes from excessive clauses:

1. He was a man who was interested in an accounting type of training.

   Shorten the sentence:

   He was interested in training in accounting.

2. The hour at which the awards ceremony will begin is three o'clock.

   Shorten the sentence:

   The awards ceremony will begin at three o'clock.

Another wasteful structure begins with "It is." Such a start will usually cause wordiness. Consider this example:

It is the judgment of this agency that steps be taken to correct the errors on the last quarterly report.

REVISION: This agency requests correction of the errors on the last quarterly report.

In the original sentence the word "it" was an indefinite word, contributing nothing to the meaning. Note how these beginnings are revised:

INSTEAD OF THIS   TRY THIS

It has now been determined ...... This agency (or this office) has decided.
It is believed .... (Change to active voice. "We believe.")
It is obvious that .... (eliminate as verbiage)
It is possible that .... may, maybe
It is recommended that consideration be given to .... We recommend that
It is requested that .... This agency (this office) requests that

Prepositional phrases can also become pet clichés of the writer. Many of these long phrases, beginning with words like <u>on</u>, <u>of</u>, <u>from</u>, <u>over</u>, <u>under</u>, <u>at</u>, <u>with</u>, etc. can be shortened to one or two words. Following the principle of reducing heavy structures, the writer can usually change phrases to single-word equivalents. This will, of course, shorten the writing. But more important, it will help to make writing strong and convincing in tone. A lengthy list of phrases follows--some may be recognized as favorite choices:

INSTEAD OF THIS	TRY THIS
Along the lines of	like
As to	about
At an early date	soon, shortly (Better yet, be specific, give the date.)
At the present time	now
At this time	now
By means of	by, with, in
Due to the fact that	because of, since, hence,
Due in large measure	because, due to
During the periods when	when
For the purpose of	for, to
For the reason that	since, because
In addition	also, besides
In a number of cases	some
In a situation in which	when
Inasmuch as	since
In a manner similar to	like
In case of	if
In compliance with	Following authority under or from
In connection with	in, with, on
In favor of	for, approve
In lieu thereof	instead
In orderly progression	in order
In order to	to
In regard to	about, concerning
In relation to	about, concerning, on, in, with
Insofar as	since, for, because
In sufficient time to	early enough
In terms of	in
In the amount of	for
In the course of	in
In the event of	if
In a majority of instances	usually
In the nature of	like
In the time of	during
In this category	this type
In view of	since
Needless to say	(always verbiage)
Of great importance	important
On a few occasions	occasionally
On behalf of	by, for
On his own initiative	individually or personally
Over the signature of	signed by
Per se	essentially, basically
Previous to	before
Pursuant to	in, under

INSTEAD OF THIS	TRY THIS
So as to	to
Subsequent to	after, next, following, later
Sufficiently in advance	early enough
Until such time as	until, whenever, then
Upon the successful completion of this project	when this project is done
With a view to	to
With due regard	for
With reference to	about, concerning, on
With regard to	about, on
With the exception of	except
With the result that	so

E. <u>Avoid Redundancy</u>

Repetition in writing can be used effectively, but a redundant expression (ineffective repetition) results in verbiage. Watch especially for the following usages:

1. Avoid using "doublets"--pairs of words having the same meaning.
   For example:

revert back	cease and desist
true facts	deeds and actions
important essentials	refuse and decline
merged together	first and foremost
new innovations	report or study
hope and trust	decide and determine
help or assistance	right and proper

2. Avoid using a general and a specific term together, if one covers the meaning of the other. For example:

eight in number	visible to the eye
round in shape	soft to the touch
spring season	surrounded on all sides
hot water heater	my personal opinion
month of July	the concensus of opinion
year of 1984	red in color

3. Avoid using comparative modifiers with words that cannot logically be compared. For example:

   nearly infinite   a baseless hoax
   practically impossible   entirely completed
   totally unique   *absolutely perfect
   somewhat complete   *a last "final" appearance
   a fatal slaying   *a very dead issue

   * phrases like the last three in the above list can sometimes be justified if used figuratively for added emphasis.

4. Avoid repeating words or phrases unnecessarily. Repetition can be effective, if used for better transition or for improved clarity. But unless the repetition has a definite function in the sentence, it results in verbiage. For example:

   Unnecessary repetition: The Chief Auditor will send the report to the appropriate officer; the appropriate officer will forward the report to the Board of Directors.

   Corrected: The Chief Auditor will send the report to his supervisor who will forward it to the Board of Directors.

   Unnecessary repetition: When the Supervisor or Deputy Supervisor is absent, documents may be signed by a substitute acting officially for the Supervisor or Deputy Supervisor.

   Corrected: In the absence of the Supervisor or Deputy Supervisor, an official substitute may sign documents.

5. Avoid Deadwood. A word or phrase that does not contribute to the meaning of the sentence is called "deadwood." Go over your sentences during the revising step to prune out the deadwood. Of course, no single method of sentence revision will remove all deadwood, but try to tighten up the expression by changing clauses to phrases, changing the position of elements, choosing better words, or just dropping useless wording. For example:

   Deadwood: Employees will proceed efficiently to reply to congressional inquiries in an expeditious manner.

   Corrected: Employees will respond to congressional inquiries promptly.

Deadwood: It is necessary that we hold a meeting with the Equal Opportunity Officer in order to make a determination about policies to be followed in the future.

Corrected: We must meet with the Equal Opportunity Officer to determine future policies.

F. Nouns As Modifiers

Writers should use their own good judgment in forming noun compounds (one noun used to modify another). Language often becomes shorter and more effective by using these noun compounds. For example:

father figure	security guard
scout leader	child care
ballet dancer	flood control

Be careful of using long strings of nouns to form compounds, especially titles. "Child Care Center" is a clear and familiar phrase, but expanded to "Exceptional Child Program Planning Care Center" the readability becomes difficult. Here it would be better to use a few more words for added clarity: "A Child Care Center to plan programs for the exceptional child." If a title carries official approval, use it freely--for example, "System Technology Enhancement Proposals." But avoid coining new ones that do not have official sanction. For example:

Confusing: Allied Chemical has adopted a plant employee benefits improvement program.

Clearer: Allied Chemical has adopted a program to improve benefits for plant employees.

Confusing: The new policies explain material replacement alternatives.

Clearer: The new program explains alternatives for material replacement.

G. Avoid Euphemisms and Inflated Language

The euphemism (a supposedly more tactful or less blunt expression) is a frequent cause of verbiage. Euphemisms usually weaken the language by avoiding the strong, clear term. Again the increasing complexity of our society has encouraged the practice of substituting more sophisticated and more important-sounding phrases for older, simpler words.

The euphemism can, of course, be used legitimately. For example, the most overwhelming fact that the living must face is death. We often try to soften the shock for the survivors by using these euphemisms: passed on, expired, gone to his rest or reward, called to a better life by his maker, etc. The funeral industry has substituted undertaker (once itself a euphemism) by mortician or funeral director. But replacing janitor with maintenance engineer may be more difficult to defend. Does the inflated title substantially change the broom pushing and mopping required on the job? If not, language is being used to inflate the job with stature it does not have.

Closely associated with the euphemism (and impelled by the same desire for more sophisticated language) is the habit of verbal inflation. Of course, we live and work in an environment of exaggerated language use. Merchandisers constantly use inflated advertising copy to influence their potential customers. The "Hollywooditis syndrome," as some have labeled it, tends to describe the trivial as colossal, stupendous, gigantic, or fantastic.

As long ago as the Eighteenth Century Dr. Samuel Johnson was worried about bloated language. Since his time many other language scholars have noted how often we replace perfectly good older words with inflated substitutes. The resulting weakening of the vocabulary, according to some, adds more and more levels between reality and the language used to describe it. For example, one writer tells of his frustration in trying to find a can or jar of olives in the supermarket labeled Small. He found this impossible, for the smallest size was called X-tra Large, then the labels went up the ladder to Jumbo, Gigantic, and Colossal. The same verbal status-seeking has caused grade inflation to become a problem in schools and colleges. Students and parents now interpret "C" grades as minimum performance. But formerly a "C" was the median grade indicating quite satisfactory mastery of the subject matter. Performance appraisal scales in government and industry are increasingly difficult to use because "average" ratings are considered a criticism. This leads, of course, to inventing levels above average with the use of inflated terms, such as above average, good, very good, superior. These in turn, will have to be replaced by other inflated terms like exceptional and phenomenal.

Here is the comment of one writer:

> "As a supervisor of military paper shufflers, I've gotten used to gobbledygook. The fact that the plain old garden-variety guardhouse is now euphemistically entitled an Air

Force Confinement Facility no longer bothers me. But I nearly fell off my chair when I discovered that my ballpoint pen was labeled: US Government Reproducing Medium."

PRINCIPLE: If you are tempted to coin a euphemism, or inflate your language, base your judgment on this question: Is the new expression likely to guide the reader closer to or farther from reality? Is "US Government Reproducing Medium" clearer and shorter than ballpoint pen?

H. Drop Cliches (overworked expression)

Cliches have lost their effectiveness through overuse. Though perhaps once original they have become stale and only clutter up writing. Cliches can hardly carry the reader safely from the Real World to the Idea World. The user of cliches often leaves his reader caught in the middle in the Verbal World. The writer should first attempt to recognize his use of well-worn language, then try to free himself from dependence upon it. The following list may contain some familiar examples:

INSTEAD OF THIS	TRY THIS
Accomplish (as in "these forms will be accomplished" or "instructions will be accomplished.")	prepare, complete, produce, do
Achieve the maximum results from	get the most from
Afford an opportunity	allow, let
After a thorough review of your report this headquarters approves the recommendations contained therein	we approve your recommendations
All information will be furnished promptly to the commander	inform the commander promptly
All these items will be broken down in separate categories	list these items by category
Are clearly indicated	are seen, shown
Are desirous of	want to
Are in receipt of	received
Attention is invited to	refer to
Augment	increase, extend, enlarge

4-13

INSTEAD OF THIS	TRY THIS
Cannot be overemphasized	(Leave out, when possible.)
Care should be taken	(Usually verbiage)
Cognizance (As in "under the cognizance of this office.")	(Usually verbiage. Be specific, say "this office does not audit travel vouchers.")
Commensurate	equal to, adequate, acceptable, satisfactory
Consideration should be given to the fact that	note that
Effect an improvement	improve
Enclosed herewith	enclosed are
Every effort will be made	(Leave out. If you intend to make an effort, say what effort, when, and where.)
Experience has indicated that	we have discovered, experienced
Fullest possible extent	thoroughly, completely
Gained from the following source	informed, revealed by
Give consideration to	consider
Implement	fulfill, carry out
Initiate (As in, "Initiate action to")	begin, start, act
Interpose no objection	I approve, we approve; I do not object, we do not object
Irrespective of the fact that	although
Is responsible for selecting	selects
Meets with our approval	we approve
Nothing above is to be construed as altering or affecting	this does not affect
Numerous instances have been reported	(Tell what instances apply to whom, when, where, and how.)
Our position in regard to your recommendation is that	your recommendation is accepted, rejected, etc.
Part (As in "error on our part")	Our error
Promulgate	announce, issue, set forth
Render such aid and assistance to the	help the ...

INSTEAD OF THIS	TRY THIS
Representatives of your headquarters	you, your representatives
Should differences of opinion occur between these officers	when these officers disagree
Take appropriate measures	acts, does
Take necessary action	act
Take whatever steps are necessary	do
The following will be adhered to insofar as practicable	do the following, if practicable
The instructions given here are to be used on temporary basis	these instructions are temporary
The fullest possible extent	the most
The operation may be accomplished most satisfactorily by using the following method	for the best results, use this method
The undersigned hereby makes application for	I want, I apply for
This is to acknowledge and thank you	thank you
This headquarters is cognizant of	we know
Wish to advise, wish to apologize	we advise, we apologize

Summary

While we should not make a fetish of achieving shortness, much verbiage can and should be removed from our writing. Dropping excess words will almost invariably improve the clarity and effectiveness of writing. This chapter has presented tested methods for writing briskly efficient, short sentences. The writer should particularly break down heavy clauses and substitute phrases or single words. Further, he should economize in his use of language by avoiding redundant, euphemistic, inflated, or clichéd expressions. Here's an appropriate quotation to end a chapter on conciseness:

The Lord's Prayer has 56 words.
Lincoln's Gettysburg Address has 266.
The Ten Commandments have 297.
The Declaration of Independence has 300.
But a government order setting the price of cabbage has 26,911 words.

Exercise 1	Chapter Four	CONCISENESS

Directions: Rearrange the elements and reduce the verbiage in these examples. Use the suggested revision method of first identifying the main ideas, then writing sentences to emphasize them:

1. The graduate work in the commerce program is designed to intensify the competence of personnel interested in preparing themselves to develop skills gained in the undergraduate field and their eventual development of supervisory positions in government and industry.

2. The different portions of the listing, though produced from the same plugboard wiring and therefore generally similar for all HQ elements, will exhibit some organizational specificity. That requirement is established by the intrinsic nature of each organizational element's work output(s) and by the extrinsic processing philosophies of the affected activity managers.

3. This Agency concurs at this time with the abandonment of modifications to the fender skirts on the subject handling units for the reason stated in paragraph 3 of the basic letter. However, for record purposes, this Agency is not in entire consonance with the author's adductions and the consequential educement of the regulation to a problem area that is opined latent.

Exercise 1--page two

4. From a HEW memo:

   Urgency is occasioned by the fact that this situation has been existent for a prolonged period of time during which no concerted effort has been made to effectuate a correction of this abuse.

5. A statement of the proposed operation of the project works during times of low, normal and flood flows on the stream, including a statement of reservoir elevations and the minimum flow proposed to be released, during the recreation season and periods of water, and, to the extent possible, full exposition of any proposed use of the project for the conservation and utilization in the public interest of the available water resources for the purposes of power, navigation, irrigation, reclamation, flood control, recreation, fish, wildlife, and municipal water supply.

Exercise 2   Chapter Four   "WORKING VERBS"

Directions: Change the following sentences to use a "working" verb instead of weak adjective and noun forms:

1. The executive has the basic responsibility of supplying top-level leadership throughout his organization.

2. It was almost midnight when the officers made the decision that the suspect should be released.

3. The Executive Committee of the Suggestion System was unable to reach a decision on the proper award to be given.

4. The Training Officer delivered a presentation on skill required in preparing and writing concise reports.

5. In the course of his communication he made a reference to their previous telephone conversation.

6. The supervisor was highly offended when his letter was given criticism at the staff meeting.

Exercise 2--page two

7. He held a lengthy conference with his assistant in order to make a determination about what the promotion policy of the organization should be.

8. When we held the meeting the Equal Opportunity Officer made a decision that Mr. Thompson should take action on this case at once.

9. The judge made the reply that the veteran should make an appearance at the hearing to furnish adequate answers to the charges.

10. He was negligent in furnishing adequate details about the duties comprising his job responsibility.

Exercise 3   Chapter Four   REDUCING STRUCTURES

Directions: In the following sentences reduce the clauses to phrases or single words.

1. Mr. Johnson, who is Chairman of the Committee, will schedule a meeting that will consider the proposal.

2. The Council, which was established by the United Nations, meets whenever matters that are crucial come up.

3. Read carefully the instructions that accompany this application so that you will be aware of the procedure that you should use.

4. The problem that is of major concern to the agency is the method that your company will use to produce the model within the time frame that you have suggested.

5. The supervisor instructed us about some new techniques that have proven successful in other organizations which have had similar problems.

Exercise 3--page two

6. He delivered his briefing that presented better production methods in a way that was both informative and entertaining.

7. They agreed that the decision would be reached during the first month that production is started.

8. The Project Manager will arrange so that you can be present at the demonstration that is scheduled for next Monday.

9. You are advised that this data is provided because this Office assumes that there will be no changes in the regulation prior to the time that you become eligible for benefits.

10. In answer to your letter of June 10 please be advised that we do not have current statistics on the labor force that is employed in the building trades but that the Department of Labor may be able to suggest a source that would be able to help you.

Exercise 4   Chapter Four   CLICHÉS

1. Can you recognize the worn-out, tired language in the following news article? It is from an old "pro" in politics whose name has been withheld to protect the guilty. Circle the clichés in the article:

> Davis Jefferson began a third term as a governor of the state today with a warning to the nation's leaders that the people "deserve and will demand" a full accounting from those responsible for a faltering economy and mismanaged government.
>
> Jefferson, in his prepared inaugural address, made no mention of what part, if any, he might play in the 1976 election. But "with an abiding interest in national affairs," he said he will "speak out when and where necessary."
>
> Jefferson has generally be regarded as a likely candidate for President again.
>
> The governor said that because of what they have seen in recent years "in both our economy and in our government, our people are discouraged, disillusioned, and disenchanted."
>
> He said Watergate has been a "traumatic experience that has left the people suspicious of government at all levels."
>
> He warned they want an accounting now, and "it is well that the leaders of government heed this message."
>
> Public officials must seek to restore confidence in government, with honesty, integrity, fair play, and a dedicated concern for the people's needs, he said.
>
> Jefferson said that to revive the shaken economy, "positive and affirmative action" must be taken to see that working men and women have jobs at decent pay without having to turn to "charitable handouts" and unnecessary new government spending.
>
> And he added, "we must see an end to artificial or contrived shortages in goods and production," resulting in "exorbitant profits."

2. Now list at least 10 phrases you have circled in the article and express them in a stronger way:

Exercise 5   Chapter Four   DOUBLETS
                                                         REPETITION
                                                         DEADWOOD

Directions: Revise the following sentences to eliminate doublets, unnecessary repetition, and deadwood.

1. Many basic and fundamental reasons lead us to the conclusion that the project will be concluded and terminated.

2. Officers will authorize and direct all requests for funding and financing which said officers determine to be within their purview and scope of authority.

3. In the case of defective material it is necessary and essential that such material, after having been deemed defective, be rejected.

4. The accounting function will take charge of and be responsible for record keeping; the function will also prepare the annual audit report.

5. Our plans and expectations are to conduct a survey and an investigation of the physical plant during the month of May.

4-23

Exercise 5--page two

6. It was discovered by the investigating committee that funds had been lost and misdirected.

7. After ignoring the research done previously, the scientist at the Center conducted a survey. The scientist wanted to gather data about public reaction to the proposed widening of the stream.

8. It is essential in the case of machinery that is not reliable in performance to prohibit and forbid its continued use.

9. The latest survey discovered that great supplies of mineral deposits in the immediate area could be expected to have the effect and the eventual result of attracting industry to the area.

10. We wish to express our disappointment and regret that you have decided to end your career and service to the Agency at this particular time.

Questions and/or Comments for Class Discussion

GOOD WRITING IS COHERENT

CHAPTER 5

PART TWO

Chapter Five--Good Writing Is Coherent

Objectives of Chapter Five:

1. To consider English as a "position" language.
2. To study connective words as an aid to coherence.
3. To point out devices for coherence in concise sentences, paragraphs, and the whole report.

Clear and concise writing needs a third very important quality for effectiveness--coherence. This gives writing strength and unity of purpose. Coherent writing impresses the reader as moving steadily toward the main points. It is smooth and emphatic and has a flowing rhythmical pattern. Coherence is a major aid toward achieving good readability.

A. <u>English as an Analytical (Position) Language</u>

The language we speak and write today is the result of centuries of development. English has consistently moved from an inflectional language (where the words change form for different uses in the sentence) to an analytical one (where position in the sentence is all-important). As a result of this change, the order of words in modern English is an important source of coherence.

For example, to a German learning English this word order seems correct: "I will throw the cow over the fence some hay." But coherence in English requires that the words be placed as follows:

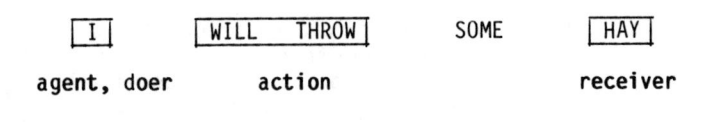

I	WILL THROW	SOME	HAY
agent, doer	action		receiver

OVER THE FENCE TO THE COW.
details (where, etc.)

Figure 6

When a Spaniard says, "The pen, I have lost her" or "The watch, he is busted" he is translating good Spanish into faulty English.

Thus, an analytical language depends for its meaning on the order of sentence elements. In fact, even in nonsense rhymes, we can recognize the function of words from their form and position. Consider this from Lewis Carroll's <u>Through the Looking Glass</u>:

> 'Twas brillig and the slithy toves
> Did gyre and gimble in the wabe.
> All mimsy were the borogroves
> And the mome raths outgrabe.

Even though apparently meaningless, the "words" can be recognized by their apparent function in the sentences:

Naming words (nouns)--brillig, toves, raths, and borogroves
Action words (verbs)--gyre, gimble, outgrabe
Measuring words (modifiers)--slithy, mimsy, mome
Connecting words (conjunctions and prepositions)--and, in

B. <u>Order of Sentence Units</u>

Because English is a position language, the readability of a sentence often depends upon where writers place modifying phrases and clauses. If too many dependent elements occur together, the sentence will usually lack strength.

EXAMPLE: Note how this incoherent sentence "dribbles" off into a weak ending:

> Personnel managers should accept the responsibility to release employees, upon supervisors' recommendation, who fail to perform their duties as an essential function of their executive position.

ANALYSIS: A number of faults can be recognized in this sentence. The main trouble stems from poor placement of phrases and clauses. The last 20 words are a succession of five dependent units confusingly linked together.

REVISION: By shifting some elements of the sentence to the middle or first position, we have a coherent statement: In their executive position, personnel managers should follow supervisors' recommendations by releasing employees who fail to perform their duties.

Strange results, indeed, can occur when phrases attach themselves to the wrong element. This headline led to some unintended humor:

ETHICS COMMITTEE CENSURES SEX BEHIND CLOSED DOORS

Sometimes deliberate changes of position in word order can be a source of humor. One comedian in the wake of the Congressional sex scandals inverted the words in a well-known popular phrase by saying: "Strange bedfellows make politics." Another showed quite an imagination in describing how a flock of birds called "terns" suddenly showed an interest in sipping from an open vat of liquor outside a distillery. He described the experience as not leaving a "tern unstoned." Winston Churchill capitalized on a deliberate contradiction in the middle of this sentence: "England and America are two countries separated by a common language."

Of course, inversion (reversing and repeating key words) can be used for more serious purposes. Who can forget, for example, President's Kennedy's challenge to the American people--"Ask not what your country can do for you: Ask what _you_ can do for your _country_!" Inverting the order of words in the second part of the sentence makes the statement memorable.

C. <u>Use of Connective Words</u>

Most of the time, however, writers are not interested in humorous or dramatic effects but in clear coherence in the sentence. In achieving this proper relationship the connective words (prepositions and conjunctions) are very important. Note how the following sentences become incoherent from one little word incorrectly used:

1. The conditions were clearly poor, <u>but</u> there was much disease among the natives.

2. He accepted the position, <u>but</u> he discharged his duties faithfully.

3. The plan had been carefully prepared, <u>and</u> in practice it was entirely unworkable.

One of the hardest lessons to teach writers is the necessity to <u>supply on paper</u> the connectives indicating relationships between ideas. As writers we often assume too much. Since the connection is clear <u>in our minds,</u> we feel it will be equally clear to the reader. To illustrate the great help these words can be, here are three common types of connection:

1. Identical Relationship--when one idea is practically the same as another.

   EXAMPLE: The report is an essential tool for the manager. It is the basis for progress in the organization.

   ANALYSIS: The two sentences could stand alone, but for better coherence they belong together.

   REVISION: The report is an essential tool for the manager, for it is the basis for progress in the organization.

2. Opposite Relationship--when one idea contradicts another.

   EXAMPLE: Learning to write better has it difficulties. You can improve if you study the text and work out the exercises.

   ANALYSIS: The sentence needs a word to show contrast between the two statements. Adding a connective clarifies the thought.

   REVISION: Learning to write better has its difficulties, but you can improve if you study the text and work out the exercises.

3. Adding-to Relationship--when a second idea says more about, illustrates, or gives an example of the first idea.

   EXAMPLE: A report should be built on an orderly fashion. Building a skyscraper must follow a plan.

   ANALYSIS: Without a connective like for example, for instance, or just as, the second sentence seems remote from the first.

   REVISION: A report should be built in an orderly fashion, just as building a skyscraper must follow a plan.

D. <u>Sentence Patterns for Coherence</u>

   1. Use proper subordination of ideas. Put main ideas in a prominent place in the sentence (usually in a main clause) and less important ideas in lesser structures (dependent clauses, phrases or single words).

FAULTY: Mr. Brown was in his first year on the job, although his judgments were often better than those of many more years experience. (The sentence places the wrong emphasis on his time on the job rather than his good judgments.)

REVISED: Although Mr. Brown was in his first year on the job, his judgments were often better than those of many more years experience.

2. Avoid excessive subordination. Too much loosely related detail in a sentence will cause it to break down under its own weight.

FAULTY: The Chief, when he is not on leave, attends the staff meeting each month which is held on the second Tuesday.

REVISED: Unless he is on leave, the Chief attends the staff meeting on the second Tuesday of each month.

3. Show clear relationships in listing items. The following sentence is faulty because it implies a three-item series:

FAULTY: In the parade there were a number of musical units, some caged animals, and a marching band.

REVISED: In the parade there were some caged animals and musical units, one of them a marching band.

4. State in your sentence all steps necessary to progress from one idea to another.

FAULTY: A court sentence may be appealed, but the evidence must be applicable to the defendant's claim.

REVISED: A court sentence may be appealed, but the appeal must be submitted with evidence applicable to the defendant's claim.

5. Try to follow the subject-verb-object (actor-action-receiver) order in sentences. If too many words are placed between these elements, they will interfere with the coherence of the sentence.

FAULTY: He, when he considered his many costly mistakes in the past, decided to accept the next available job.

REVISED: After considering his many costly mistakes in the past, he decided to accept the next available job.

FAULTY: The reports must include, upon submission to the appropriate agency, estimated costs, time schedules, and a projected overview.

REVISED: Upon submission to the appropriate agency, the reports must include estimated costs, time schedules, and a projected overview.

6. Use parallel structure (balanced construction) to present ideas in a clear and orderly way. Parallel structure <u>must be used</u> for expressing two or more thoughts equal in importance. Of course, it should not be used if the ideas are not equally important. The following sentence patterns require parallel structure:

   a. When you connect words, phrases, or clauses with equality connectives (coordinating conjunctions). The English language contains only six of these words: <u>and</u>, <u>but</u>, <u>for</u>, <u>or</u>, <u>nor</u>, <u>so</u>. When you use one of these, consider it like an equal (=) sign and check the elements on each side for parallelism.

   FAULTY: This new product offers easy operation, economy, and is simple to install.

   REVISED: This new product offers easy operation, economy, and simple installation.

   b. When you use double connectives (correlatives) to join elements. These are expressions used in pairs like <u>either...or</u>, <u>not only...but also</u>, etc.

   FAULTY: It was not only Smith's poor test scores that disqualified him but also he didn't have enough experience in the field.

   REVISED: Not only Smith's poor test scores but also his lack of experience disqualified him.

   c. When you present items in a series or when you use symbols (1, 2, 3, or a, b, c) in front of lists.

   FAULTY: Three steps must be followed in this process:
   (1) Remove dirt and rust from the metal
   (2) Put the pipes through an acid bath
   (3) Then you should cut the pipes into the desired lengths

REVISED: Three steps must be followed in this process:
       (1) Remove dirt and rust from the metal
       (2) Put the pipes through an acid bath
       (3) Cut the pipes into the desired lengths

   d. When you make comparisons in the sentence using "as" or "than."

FAULTY: Cleaning with acid is easier than to grind off the rust.

REVISED: Cleaning with acid is easier than grinding off the rust.

7. Use active voice, where possible, instead of passive. In most sentences the active verb will be more direct and less wordy than the passive construction. Active voice is easier to understand because it places sentence elements in this order: actor-action-receiver.

   EXAMPLE: Jack threw the ball. (active)
                  The ball was thrown by Jack. (passive)

<u>Why say this</u>?--A determined effort must be made by our entire staff to cut our expenses.

<u>When you could say this</u>--Our entire staff must make a determined effort to cut expenses.

The passive voice can be especially fuzzy when it hides responsibility for an action.

<u>Why say this</u>?--A mistaken estimate of sales potential was made in last year's market report.

<u>When you could say this</u>?--The market analysts mistakenly estimated last year's sales potential.

Generally there is far too much use of the passive voice. Strangely enough, some courses in writing have encouraged its use to achieve an impersonal tone. But impersonal writing seems remote from the reader and lacks the YOU attitude. Sometimes, of course, the passive voice must be used. For example, for the following purposes the passive voice is effective:

   a. To emphasize the action or the doer of the action by placement at the end of the sentence.

EXAMPLE: Measures for overcoming the energy shortage are approved only the Commission Chairman. (emphasizes the required approval by the Chairman)

   b. To phrase a sentence when the doer of the action is unknown.

EXAMPLE: The method was first used in England during the Nineteenth Century.

8. Use variety in sentence length and arrangement to make your writing more attractive and readable. In number 5 above the subject-verb-object arrangement was recommended as the best. You can, however, follow the SVO pattern and still enjoy much freedom in arranging the dependent elements in the sentence.

   PRINCIPLE: Usually the skilled writer will try to vary the order of sentence elements because this makes writing easier to read.

   Here are three different ways that the sentence above could have been expressed:

a. The skilled writer will usually try to vary the order of sentence elements because this makes writing easier to read.

b. Because variety makes writing easier to read, the skilled writer will try to vary the order of sentence elements.

c. To achieve easier readability, the skilled writer will vary the order of sentence elements.

   ANALYSIS: In the various versions of the sentence above, "b" and "c" are better arrangements. Unless some special effect is desired, the ideas of lesser importance ought to be expressed first or in the middle; this will allow the writer to express the main idea in the most emphatic position--the end of the sentence.

   Sentence lengths should also be varied to avoid monotony. While the experts have cited 17-21 words as the _average_ sentence length, this does not rule out using an occasional longer sentence or a very short one.

Longer sentences can be used effectively to gather together a number of details or supporting reasons.

EXAMPLE: For the following reasons I support a change in our accounting procedures: (1) _____, (2) _____, (3) _____, etc.

Note: Any number of items could be accommodated efficiently in such a listing.

A short sentence among longer ones will always call attention to itself. Therefore, if you wish to emphasize <u>one</u> idea over all others in a paragraph, phrase it in a short sentence.

EXAMPLE: (Note the emphasis placed upon the last short sentence.)

    Living in this modern age of technical progress, we must receive adequate training in the technical fields. Almost everyone, even our most ardent supporters of the liberal arts, do not deny this. However, although ours is a technical civilization, technical knowledge is not enough. Something more is needed to help us meet our problems. That <u>something</u> is general education.

9. Combine ideas for better coherence. The subject and the verb are really all we need to express an idea in a sentence. But a sentence often needs to combine several items of information within its structure to make the relationship among them clear. Consider the following six sentences:

The army continued on. They traveled as rapidly as possible. At dusk they stopped. They pitched camp. The site was by a lake. The lake was in the mountains.

ANALYSIS: The statements need to be combined in order to avoid the interruptive, choppy style. Indeed one mark of a mature writer is the ability to choose sentence structures effectively in order to show coherent relationships among ideas. Using the example above, the writer first decides upon the subject idea (army), second, the verb idea (pitched camp). Then the other information is worked into the sentence using dependent structures. Here is the combined sentence:

AFTER	TRAVELING	AS RAPIDLY AS POSSIBLE	UNTIL DUSK,
time word	verbal phase	adverb modifier	phrase

THE ARMY	PITCHED	CAMP	BESIDE A MOUNTAIN LAKE.
subject	verb	object	phrase

E. <u>Coherence of the Paragraph</u>

The paragraph has often been the forgotten unit in training for better writing. Yet the paragraph is the key to coherence, for, rightly used, it can effectively organize the phases of thought in the larger message. Correct order of sentences, properly connected within the paragraph, can virtually insure the clarity and coherence of the message.

First of all, let us examine the basic structure of a well-formed paragraph. The most tightly organized paragraph might be illustrated as follows:

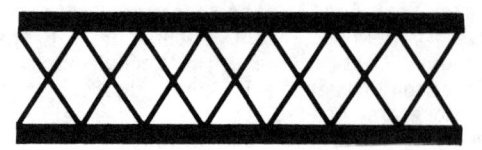

TOPIC SENTENCE

SUPPORTING MATERIAL

SUMMARY SENTENCE

Figure 7

The lines crossing each other show the need for transition among the supporting sentences.

Some writers have labeled this type the "sandwich" paragraph. Just as an actual sandwich is made with a top and a bottom piece of bread and filler in between, this type of paragraph encloses its message. The topic and the summary sentences express the general idea, and the sentences in between support and develop it. Writers need not include a final summary sentence with every paragraph, for this could result in mere repetition of idea. <u>The topic sentence, however, should always be included.</u> Thus, the "sandwich" type paragraph can be almost a fail-safe guarantee of clarity and coherence.

Now reread the last paragraph and notice the "sandwich" development used. The first sentence introduces the term, the following sentences develop the thought, and the final sentence summarizes the message of the paragraph.

CAUTION: Reserve the fully developed "sandwich" paragraph for expressing only the most important ideas in a memo or report. In a report under five pages, three or four are usually enough.

Now let us further explain the other terms used in the diagram above.

The topic sentence. Except in rare instances, this should be first in the paragraph. Many texts on composition take a much more liberal view, maintaining that the topic sentence can occur at any point in the paragraph. But the reader will find it easier to follow your writing if you regularly place it first. Someone has defined the topic sentence as "telling what the paragraph is about, but not telling everything about the paragraph." That's not double talk--it's a good working definition. This first sentence should be general, an introductory "umbrella" type of statement to ease the reader into the paragraph unit. Without it, there will be an abrupt, hard-to-follow quality in the writing.

The middle sentences. These develop and support the topic of the paragraph. They should be linked to the first sentence and to each other by verbal or logical connection. Here are some ways to achieve better coherence within a paragraph:

1. Verbal connectives
    a. Repeated words (usually the main words in the topic sentence)
    b. Pronouns--it, they, he, etc.
    c. Pointer words--this, that, these, those, such
    d. Transition words--further, however, similarly, but, though, etc.

2. Logical connection refers to the natural flow of thought from one sentence to the next. In paragraphs developed according to a "time" or "space" order (see section H below) there is often a natural coherence. But if you have any doubt about the paragraph unity, put in some verbal connectives. These can be added right up to the time of the final draft.

The summary sentence. On very important paragraphs you should consider adding a last sentence as a summary statement. Since the summary sentence restates the main idea contained in the topic sentence, it can provide a double assurance of the message getting through. Because the paragraph idea has been supported by the middle sentences, the summary will, of course, be a more fully developed statement than the topic sentence.

Here is a sample paragraph with the devices for coherence pointed out:

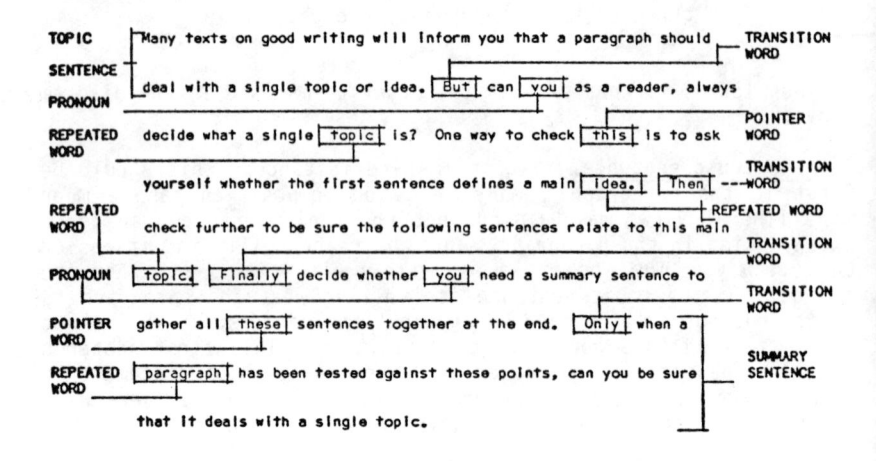

```
TOPIC          Many texts on good writing will inform you that a paragraph should      TRANSITION
SENTENCE                                                                               WORD
               deal with a single topic or idea. But can you as a reader, always
PRONOUN
                                                                                       POINTER
REPEATED       decide what a single topic is? One way to check this is to ask          WORD
WORD
                                                                                       TRANSITION
               yourself whether the first sentence defines a main idea. Then ---WORD
REPEATED                                                                    REPEATED WORD
WORD           check further to be sure the following sentences relate to this main
                                                                                       TRANSITION
                                                                                       WORD
PRONOUN        topic. Finally decide whether you need a summary sentence to
                                                                                       TRANSITION
                                                                                       WORD
POINTER        gather all these sentences together at the end. Only when a
WORD
                                                                                       SUMMARY
REPEATED       paragraph has been tested against these points, can you be sure         SENTENCE
WORD
               that it deals with a single topic.
```

Figure 8

F. Lists of Transitional Words

The sample paragraph above shows the great value of transition words in tying your thoughts together. The following lists will further indicate how many expressions are available for this purpose:

1. To point forward or to show contrast

    in order that
    so that
    then
    first, second, finally, etc.
    in fact
    for example
    furthermore
    further
    next
    soon
    presently
    shortly

2. To show contrast

    but
    different from
    and yet
    however
    nevertheless
    on the contrary
    on the other hand
    in spite of
    still
    although, though
    notwithstanding

3. To point backward

   This plan showed
   These data suggest
   The latter idea shows
   The above-mentioned criteria
   From this factor
   As cited earlier
   Meanwhile
   Formerly, we cited

4. To show similarity

   similarly
   likewise
   comparable to
   analogous to
   identical to
   in the same way
   just as

5. To show result

   accordingly
   consequently
   therefore
   thus
   in short
   to conclude
   of course
   in summary
   hence
   in brief
   as a result
   for this reason
   then
   since

6. To show concession

   after all
   at the same time
   naturally
   of course
   as a matter of principle
   will concede that
   agree in principle that

Of course, these are not complete lists but they may suggest some available expressions to show relationships between ideas.

G. The Transitional Paragraph

To secure needed coherence between the sections of a memo or report, you may need a separate transitional paragraph. This type of paragraph is not arranged in the usual topic-sentence-plus-development fashion, for its only function is to bring together the larger sections of a piece of writing. If you are writing from an outline (and it is risky not to!), you may need a transitional paragraph in moving from one main point to the next.

For an example of a transitional paragraph look back to page 3-13 of Chapter Three--Good Writing is Clear. The last paragraph on that page is designed to lead ahead to Chapter Four. In long, complex reports you may need to include such paragraphs of transition. They are simple to write--merely tell the reader what you have done in the previous section and what you are going to do in the next. Being familiar with the material, the writer may not be aware of the need for transitional paragraphs. But the reader often needs this extra help in getting from one section of the report to the next.

EXAMPLE:

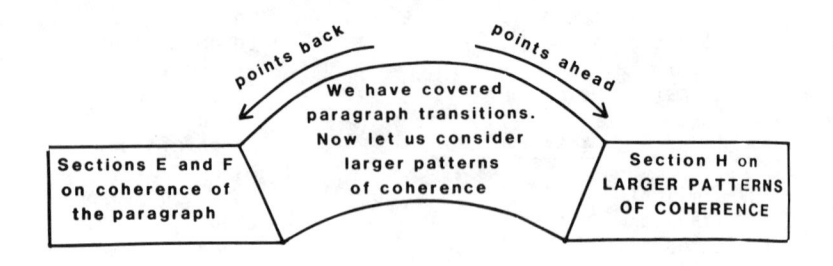

```
     points back                    points ahead
   ┌──────────────┐ ┌──────────────────┐ ┌──────────────┐
   │ Sections E and F │ │ We have covered  │ │  Section H on │
   │  on coherence of │ │ paragraph transitions. │ │ LARGER PATTERNS │
   │  the paragraph   │ │ Now let us consider │ │  OF COHERENCE │
   │                  │ │  larger patterns │ │              │
   │                  │ │   of coherence   │ │              │
   └──────────────────┘ └──────────────────┘ └──────────────┘
```

Figure 9

II. Patterns of Coherence in the Report

Of course, there are as many different ways of organizing the material in a report as there are writers. In this section on patterns in report writing, therefore, we will be doing some generalizing. Here is an outline of some organizational patterns to be discussed in detail in the rest of this chapter:

1. Inductive patterns
   a. Time order
   b. Space order
   c. Introduction-Body-Conclusion order
2. Deductive pattern--the "executive" report
3. Other organizational patterns

Let us first examine the terms used opposite numbers 1 and 2 above--Inductive and Deductive.

The *Inductive* method follows the natural order of the thinking process--first gathering data, facts, instances, etc., then coming to a conclusion. Induction has been the method of modern science from the time of Francis Bacon in the Sixteenth Century to the present. As Bacon pointed out, many errors in thinking occur because of pre-conceived conclusions, arrived at before sufficient evidence is available.

The Deductive method, on the other hand, refers to the opposite kind of presentation--starting with the conclusions or results, then working back to the supporting material--examples, causes, details, etc.

Writers should realize clearly that deductive order refers only to the method chosen to present material in a memo or report. It does not refer to the thought process leading to a conclusion. Good researchers come to conclusions and recommendations by gathering evidence inductively. But they often choose to state the results of their research first, then to record how they arrived at those conclusions. Deduction merely presents material in the opposite order from the normal thinking process to save time for the reader.

The two methods are illustrated below:

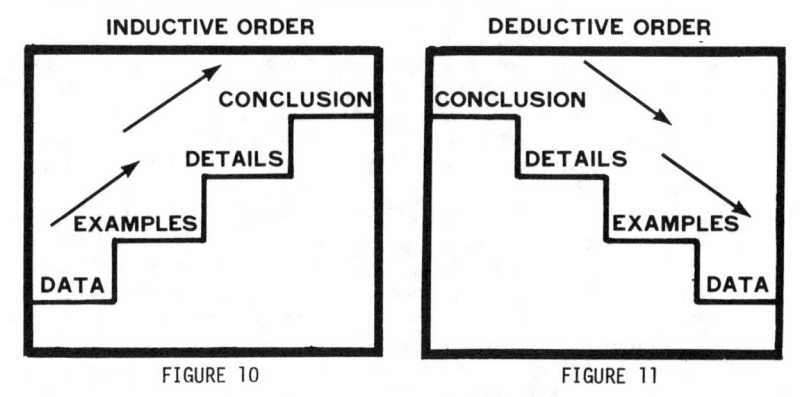

INDUCTIVE ORDER   **DEDUCTIVE ORDER**

```
         CONCLUSION           CONCLUSION
       DETAILS                  DETAILS
   EXAMPLES                          EXAMPLES
 DATA                                    DATA
```

FIGURE 10   FIGURE 11

Now let us examine in detail the three types of inductive development:

1. Inductive Patterns

    a. Time Order: We are all tied to time--events occur in sequence, but only special kinds of subject matter should be presented in order of time. Reports of industrial accidents and fires probably require a time order, at least for the information report. Even here, however, when the purpose is to determine causes, the writer should consider another arrangement (in order of cause to effect or perhaps from most likely cause to least likely). Trip reports, for example, are not ordinarily well organized according to a time sequence. Look at this beginning:

>As instructed I sent in a registration form with the required information for the Computer Programming Seminar. After being accepted I attended the conference at the Conrad Hilton Hotel in Chicago on March 21-25. At the seminar I found it hard to select the best panel discussion for our needs. However, the series on "Training Programs for Career Service Employees" was the highlight of the conference, etc.

COMMENT: The report should have begun (after a short introduction) with the last sentence--the time order was ineffective. The temptation to follow chronology is great because it's easy--easy, that is, for the writer--but often incoherent for the reader.

b.   *Space Order*: Be likewise careful about developing your report around a step-by-step or space order. (Space order follows a development according to the physical or geographical arrangement of items.) For a topic such as "How the X Computer Operates," the step-by-step arrangement following the operations of the machine, may be your only choice. But then perhaps your supervisor really wants to know how it will serve *your* accounting needs best, what efficiency it will bring to *your* record-keeping, etc. Wouldn't these purposes dictate a different plan? In purely informational type reports on, for instance, a logistics subject or a description of a shop procedure, the space order is appropriate. Conclusions, recommendations and/or a summary should be included at the end of reports developed according to a space order. Otherwise the reader may have trouble recalling the steps presented in the study.

COMMENT: Since the emphasis in this book has been on THINKING before writing, we should think carefully before choosing a time or space order of development. Many reviewers of correspondence agree that telling it just as it happened or just as it exists in space often interferes with reader understanding. Coherent writers choose these patterns only when:

(1) The time or space order is essential for the clarity of the presentation.

(2) Supervisors or other readers insist upon these organizational patterns.

c. <u>Introduction</u>-<u>Body</u>-<u>Conclusion</u> <u>Order</u>: (the basic inductive pattern) This order might be illustrated by a figure like the following:

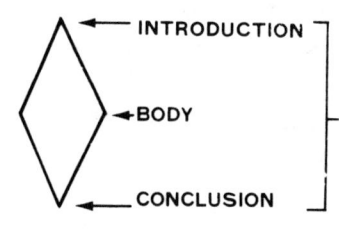

```
  /\   ←——— INTRODUCTION  ⎤
 /  \                      ⎥     The report begins slowly,
 \  /  ←—BODY              ⎬    presents data in the middle;
  \/                       ⎥     then logically comes to
  /\  ←——— CONCLUSION      ⎦         the conclusions.
```

Figure 12

This pattern follows the oldest, and the wisest, advice about communication ever written. It goes back to Aristotle, who outlined a successful speech as having a beginning, a middle, and an end.

The success of this pattern is well illustrated in a story told about an old Southern preacher. In interviewing him a reporter asked how he managed to attract great crowds to hear his sermons. He replied, "First I tell 'em what ah'm gonna tell 'em. Then ah tell 'em. Then ah tell 'em what I told 'em." He followed an introduction-body-conclusion pattern.

The number of reports with abrupt beginnings or without summaries reveals the wisdom of checking for a beginning, a middle, and an end!

Choosing to develop your report by this method somewhat depends upon the type of reader you are addressing. If he is the rather thorough, methodical type who wants to follow your own reasoning point by point, the Introduction-body-conclusion Order would be the best choice. But when you are writing for someone used to delegating authority and accepting the recommendations of his subordinates, the "executive" pattern, described in the next paragraph may be the best.

2. <u>Deductive</u> <u>Pattern</u> (the "Executive" Report) Increasingly, busy managers are asking for deductively developed reports. These save reading time because the results or recommendations of the research are presented close to the beginning of the report. This diagram illustrates the deductive order:

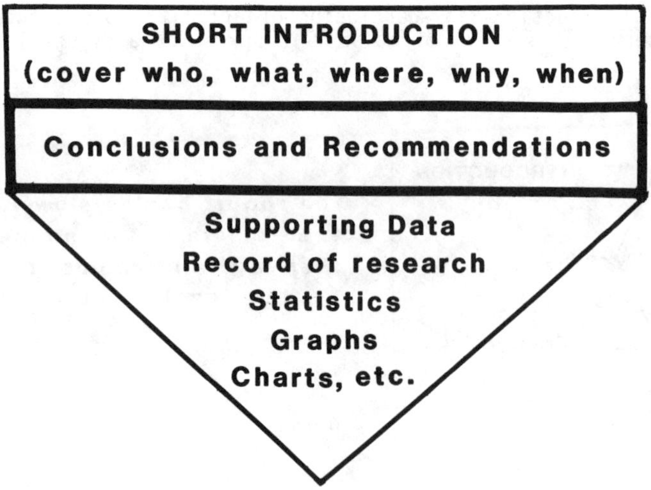

```
┌─────────────────────────────────────┐
│        SHORT INTRODUCTION           │
│  (cover who, what, where, why, when)│
├─────────────────────────────────────┤
│    Conclusions and Recommendations  │
└─────────────────────────────────────┘
    ╲         Supporting Data       ╱
     ╲       Record of research    ╱
      ╲         Statistics        ╱
       ╲          Graphs         ╱
        ╲      Charts, etc.     ╱
         ╲                     ╱
          ╲_____╱
```

Figure 13

The executive report, however, must avoid abruptness at the beginning. Such a start as the following would almost certainly confuse the reader:

SUBJECT: In-service Training Program for Career Employees

    We should radically change our present training program, based on the innovative techniques presented in a recent seminar . . . .

This may be a justified conclusion all right, but readers need more background data leading up to your proposal.

To avoid leaving the reader in the dust, write a short introduction covering such questions as these:

    Who ordered the research?
    What time-span is covered?
    Who are involved (either in the research or implementing, or both)?
    What conclusions are suggested?
    What do these conclusions mean to us?

Including these points might make the beginning less abrupt, as follows:

SUBJECT: In-service Training Programs for Career Employees

> This report presents recent developments in Training Programs for career employees. Authorized by Mr. Ernest Trainer, the data were mainly reported in a seminar at the Chicago Regional Center from 16 August to 23 August and cover research over the last two years. One particular plan is well suited to our Personnel and Training Division--The Practical Career Training Plan. We recommend its use as the best plan to improve the results of training at our agency. This will involve concurrences from the following supervisors: . . . .

3. <u>Other Organizational Patterns</u>:

    a. To avoid abrupt beginnings, some government agencies and business firms require writers to list information on a pre-printed form with headings such as the following:

> Purpose--
> Scope--
> Personnel Involved--
> Findings--
> Conclusions and Recommendations--
> Supporting Data--

Such forms encourage writers to include pertinent material in a logical order leading to their conclusions:

    b. Another practical plan can be used in a <u>persuasive</u> memo, letter, or report: Note how the steps follow logically to serve these objectives: get attention, create interest, prove feasibility, and stimulate action:

Get the ATTENTION and INTEREST of the reader with a strong, direct opening sentence:

"We have a critical need for a program to upgrade the writing skills of our employees. The efficiency of our agency depends on it."

CONVINCE the reader by an appeal to the factual not the emotional. Relate the facts to the reader's own interests and point up the seriousness of the problem:

"Continued criticism of our writing has been noted in (a) three memos from top management, (b) frequent errors in the mechanics of English found in a recent random sampling, and (c) five articles in professional journals concerning the need to upgrade communication skills."

Prove FEASIBILITY by showing how your plan is a practical solution for the problem and how the reader will benefit from your proposal:

"We believe that the problem can be addressed by offering an in-service training course in Effective Writing. But first we need your cooperation in developing a plan to serve your employees' needs."

Stimulate ACTION by making it easy for the reader to respond. If you provide clear directions about what to do, the reader is more likely to reply:

"You can be of great help to our company and get the program moving by completing the attached survey form. Please note that the questionnaire asks you to assess the quality of the writing in your office by 1 November. We will send you the survey results and keep you posted on the plan as it develops."

c. A writer can also use the 5 W's and the H of the newspaper writer: **WHO, WHAT, WHERE, WHEN, WHY, and HOW.**

Before preparing your final draft of a document, check your material using these questions:

WHO...Who are involved? Who will do the work? Who should be on the mailing list?

WHAT...What is the main concern of the reader? What will he need to know?

WHERE...Where are the locations involved? Where should the information be sent?

WHEN...When should the project be completed? Is there a deadline date or a target date? Has the plan allowed enough time for the steps to be completed?

WHY...Why is this project being presented? Is this purpose fully covered in terms of the reader's background and interests?

HOW...How will the project be completed? Financing clear? How is the reader likely to react to the proposal?

d. Finally, for extensive reports and research studies the sections are usually expanded to include:

(1) a letter of transmittal--refers to the enclosed report and the purpose for it.

(2) the abstract--condenses a long report and refers in brief (usually one or two pages) to the purpose, the scope, the personnel involved, and the conclusions presented.

(3) the report proper--contains the support material, such as the details of the study, statistics, charts, graphs, and other data to support the conclusions.

I. Four Steps in Developing a Coherent Report

Now we will examine a method of developing a report from a purpose statement to the finished product. Remember this is only one of the methods that could be used--it may not fit the needs of every writer, but it is a systematic procedure. It's at least worth trying before you decide to use another. You will come up with coherent piece of writing using this plan, and it may save you time.

1. Writing a Purpose Statement

a. General Purpose: Decide how you want the report to affect the reader. Are you writing (1) to direct, (2) to inform, or (3) to persuade? Now apply the 5 W's and H used by the news writer--who, what, where, when, why, and how. Generally a directive emphasizes what is to be done, informative writing how to do something, and persuasive writing why something should be done. Of course, the general purposes can overlap. For example, when you give information for the purpose of convincing the reader, you may have to include data under who, what, where, and when as well. Or when you describe in a directive what is to be done, part of your job may be to explain first why it must be done. Or you could say that most writing is for the "why" purpose of getting the reader on your side, that is, convincing him of the logic of your ideas. Let us say, then, that for this particular report your purpose is to PERSUADE. Presuming that this is your first contact with the reader on the subject, you will have to emphasize WHY your ideas should be accepted.

b. Specific Purpose: Once you have isolated the general purpose of the writing, phrase a specific purpose sentence. Don't trust your memory in this step; write it out in a complete statement. Two important purposes will be served by this practice: (1) a clear statement will lead to clear and coherent writing. If it is fuzzy in your mind, watch out! If it is not clear to you, it will not be clear to anyone. (2) A clearly stated specific purpose will serve as a useful "check" sentence. Data not supporting or developing the purpose statement should be discarded.

EXAMPLES:

(1) My purpose is to secure an appropriation of $12,000 to fund a program to upgrade writing skills in our organization. (This sentence seems to miss the real purpose of the report.)

(2) My purpose is to persuade the reader that we need a practical program designed to upgrade the writing skills of our employees. (This revision pinpoints the principal purpose of the writing.)

2. Developing the Main Ideas

When your specific purpose has been clarified and stated, gather material to support the purpose statement. Since this is to be a persuasive report, the reader will want to know why he should agree with you. In this data-gathering step the material may come to mind in the order of its importance. If it doesn't, don't worry--you can rearrange it in the next step--outlining.

EXAMPLE:

(Why?)   Survey shows 35% of correspondence being returned for revision.

(Why?)   Last month 20 requests for clarification were received on reports from this office.

(Why?)   Greater expense is involved in providing training at other locations.

(Why?)   At present local training facility offers no courses in Effective Writing.

(Why?)   Trade journal articles continue to point out need for offering in-service training in better communication.

(Why?)   Memos from top-level executives cite poor writing in our agency.

(Why?)   Random sampling of file material reveals much poor writing in memos and reports.

(How?)   Have our training officer investigate communications departments at local colleges. Select an instructor to develop classroom materials to serve our needs. Appoint a coordinator for the program from our training staff.

3. Arranging an Outline

    Before attempting to arrange these items, you should decide which method of development, inductive or deductive, you wish to use. This choice will affect the method of presenting material. Here is an outline evolved from the notes recorded in Step 2:

a. Statement of the problem--expand upon specific purpose statement
b. Analysis of the problem
    (1) Statistical evidence of serious need for training
        (a) 35% of correspondence returned for revision
        (b) 20 requests for clarification on reports
        (c) 3 memos from executive level

       (2) Other evidence of need for training
          (a) Random sampling of file material
          (b) Trade journals emphasizing communication skills
  c. Possible solutions for the problem
       (1) Training at other locations
       (2) No courses presently offered by Training Office
       (3) Existing courses at local colleges
  d. Recommended solution
       (1) Course to be developed here to suit our needs
       (2) Appoint a coordinator from our staff to contact our training office.
  e. Disadvantages of plan proposed
       (1) Evaluation procedures
       (2) Possible merger with Chicago facility

4. **Writing from the Outline**

    Following is a short report developed from the data in the preceding steps:

TO: David Brown, Supervisor

FROM: James Blake, Staff Assistant

SUBJECT: Upgrading Writing Skills

1. COMMENT:
Part a. in outline. Expands specific purpose statement. Refers to recommendation made later. Follows deductive order.

We have a continuing need for a program to upgrade the writing skills of our employees. Criticism has been increasing about the poor correspondence produced in our agency. We propose to solve this problem by offering training in Effective Writing sponsored by our Training Office in cooperation with Smith College. To finance the program an appropriation of $12,000 will be needed to train 20 employees during the next fiscal year. This amount will cover the costs of developing the course, instruction and printing of materials.

2. COMMENT:

Analysis of problem. Note that items b.(1)(a) and b.(1)(b) were combined in one paragraph.

The problem of poor writing here is seriously impairing our communications. Last month, for example, a survey revealed that 35% of the correspondence over one page in length was returned to the writer for major revision. Also during last month we had 20 requests for further clarification of reports issued by our office. All of these requests resulted from "fuzzy" writing, not from a lack of proper data.

3. COMMENT:

Further analysis of problem. Uses a separate paragraph to develop and emphasize item b.(1)(c) from outline.

Further evidence of continued dissatisfaction with our writing can be noted in three separate memos from top-level executives. All of these concerned the need for clearer, shorter, and more coherent writing. At the end of this report we have included a copy of one memo produced here. We have noted the many errors in mechanics of English and proper sentence structure.

4. COMMENT:

Continued analysis. Combines items b.(2)(a) and b.(2)(b).

Other factors point to the real need we have for help in raising the quality of our writing. Every sixty days for the past year we have taken from the files a random sampling of our correspondence. The kinds of errors found are summarized in an exhibit at the end of this report. Also during the past year five articles have appeared in the trade journals in our field emphasizing the importance of upgrading communications. A copy of one of these articles is included at the end of this report.

5. COMMENT:

Item c. in outline. Shows that writer has considered options. Both are more expensive and would not meet training needs.

We have investigated other possible solutions for the problem. These alternatives are referred to in the following table:

Source of Training	Cost per employee	Total cost (for 20 employees)
Communications Institutes (nearest in Chicago)	$800	$16,000
Courses at local colleges	$650	$13,000

We believe that our particular difficulties in writing would be hard to correct by courses offered elsewhere. We have examined the outlines for college courses in this type of training and find their level too advanced. None of the courses currently offered by the Training facility here are in the communications area.

6. COMMENT:

Part d. in outline. Key Paragraph. Features the best plan to meet the problem. Note careful detail and listing of steps. Previous paragraphs have prepared reader to accept the proposed plan.

We suggest that our Division develop a "tailor-made" course to upgrade our skills in writing. To accomplish this, three steps should be taken:
a. Select a person from our group to act as a coordinator to work with Training facility.
b. Contact college personnel in the Communications Department at Smith College. This institution has been recommended by six of our employees who have taken evening courses there.
c. Authorize a coordinator, a Staff Assistant in Training, and a consultant from the college to plan a course to meet our needs.

7. **COMMENT**:

Part e. in outline. Mentions possible disadvantages to present a more objective approach. It's better to face opposition head-on.

Two possible disadvantages of the proposal should be recognized. First, recovery of the cost of the program through improved writing will be difficult to measure. Careful records will have to be kept on the number of revisions required and on complaints received after completion of the training. Second, the anticipated merger with the Chicago office may increase our personnel here by 200%. This may mean added training expense and perhaps different training needs for the new employees. However, plans for the merger are apparently uncertain at this time.

8. **COMMENT**:

Last paragraph re-emphasizes the plan. Refers the reader back to first paragraph and to Key paragraph 6.

We recommend, therefore, that the plan outlined in paragraph 6 be adopted and that $12,000 be allocated to support it. We believe the advantages to be gained outweigh the possible disadvantages and that the plan is the best way to meet a serious communications problem.

Summary

We began this chapter with a special consideration of English as a "position" language. Then we looked at connective words as special helps for coherence in writing. Finally, we considered methods to improve the coherence of sentences, paragraphs, and the whole report.

Exercise 1   Chapter Five   COHERENCE

Directions: Improve the arrangement of elements within these sentences. Try to shorten them too, for added improvement:

1. It is most important that a time be set aside, during this bicentennial year for Americans to recognize the important contributions made to our nation's life, history, and culture by our black citizens.

2. The AMA study indicates that it is difficult to spot a potential absentee before he becomes one because in many cases his absenteeism is a function of how he feels about the job and his illnesses may be psychosomatically induced by his hatred of the job.

3. The Colonel's face showed no emotion but anxiety and a little nervousness must have been hiding behind that impassive expression on his face.

4. The Personnel Chief rejected the application from James because he was not friendly toward him.

Exercise 1--page two

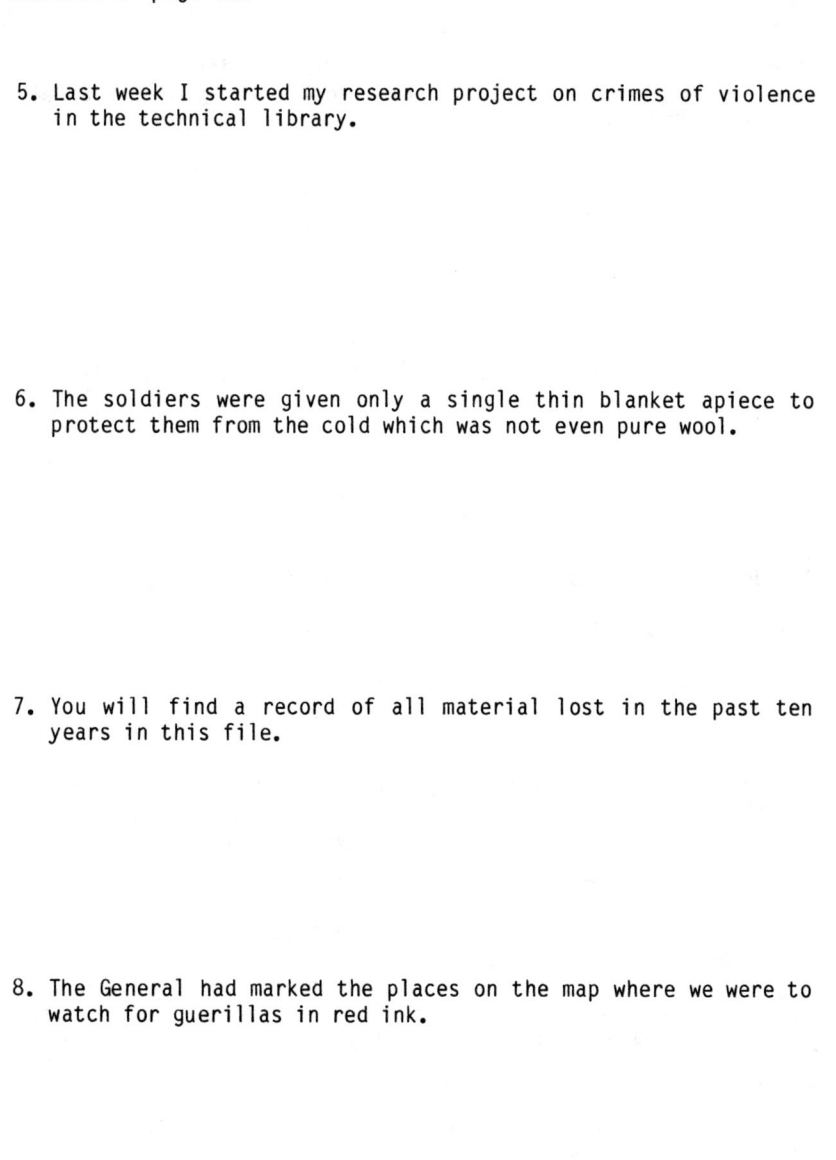

5. Last week I started my research project on crimes of violence in the technical library.

6. The soldiers were given only a single thin blanket apiece to protect them from the cold which was not even pure wool.

7. You will find a record of all material lost in the past ten years in this file.

8. The General had marked the places on the map where we were to watch for guerillas in red ink.

Exercise 2   Chapter Five   COHERENCE

Directions: The following sentences could be improved by better subordination, clearer relationships, or better position of elements. Rewrite each sentence.

1. Since we acquired more data by the complete survey in two weeks, we were able to submit the final report.

2. The shredder that she had been running noisily fell from the platform.

3. When the fire broke out and destroyed the warehouse, he was busily processing the data.

4. The performance appraisal which must be conducted annually will be signed by the employee who is being rated in the department where the rating applies.

5. Many employees stay with the firm for years, the new stock purchase plan is an added incentive.

Exercise 2--page two

6. This calculator operates on an entirely new principle, it is based on three years of research.

7. Since rejected suggestions may be reconsidered, further data on cost-saving can be presented.

8. The office was equipped with filing cabinets, business machines, an inter-com system, and an electric typewriter.

9. This report, in accordance with the regulation applying to such documents, has been submitted to the Director.

10. Unless careful records are maintained, the project will lack, as has so often happened in the past, the support of the staff.

Exercise 3   Chapter Five   PARALLEL STRUCTURE

Directions: Rephrase the following sentences to make them parallel in structure.

1. Our staff people are expected to be on travel about four days each month, to submit reports after each trip, and they must make out daily expense records.

2. All trainees are given instruction in operating visual aid equipment and how to write staff reports.

3. The supervisor should have the ability to plan or getting things done.

4. Planning a report is often as hard as to write it.

5. Our service offers vocational training courses, assists in job placement, and it sponsors a series of employment seminars.

6. Both the supervisory personnel and including the shop workers favored becoming unionized.

Exercise 3--page two

7. The inspector demanded to see the memo and that he be allowed to search the premises.

8. The Central Office arranges recreational activities; it also takes care of conferences, and moreover the lecture series is its job.

9. It is worse to plan a report poorly than give an incoherent order orally.

10. Richard Cory is a person of great potential in our agency but who may not have the requisite education and experience for the job.

11. In our last letter we requested the following:
    a. a financial statement
    b. a list of credit references
    c. we also asked for the name of your bank

Exercise 3--page three

12. Four steps are necessary for successful writing:
    a. To think carefully about the subject
    b. Then you should outline your data
    c. To write a first draft hastily
    d. Be sure that you revise your copy

13. The supervisor gave us instructions on office procedures and also to show us proper dress for working hours and third he went over forms used in the agency.

14. Persuasive writing should be organized as follows:
    a. Gain attention
    b. Interest the reader
    c. Produce conviction
    d. You should create desire for the product or service
    e. Efforts in the direction of getting action from the reader

15. We received a large order in October and which was increased in November.

Exercise 4   Chapter Five   ACTIVE VOICE

Directions: If possible, in the following sentences change the passive verb to active voice for better directness:

1. It is suggested by the Executive Committee that the employees contribute to the United Fund.

2. Members of our agency are encouraged by the Personnel Manager to contribute to this worthy cause.

3. It is the belief of the company president that the problem is caused by lack of sufficient personnel.

4. At the close of the business day, receipts should be tallied and reported to the Chief Accountant.

5. It was reported that the employees were circulating a petition asking for the right to bargain collectively.

6. We use overhead projectors in the first two classrooms, and slide projectors are provided in the other two.

Exercise 4--page two

7. Many years ago a similar error was made in recording the proper personnel data.

8. Permission for changes in vacation schedules must be approved only by your immediate supervisor.

9. It is hoped by the Chairman that this clears up any possible misunderstanding.

10. It is the judgment of this Agency that an office newsletter be established so that items of interest can be reported each week.

Exercise 5   Chapter Five   COMBINING SENTENCES

Directions: Combine each group of sentences below into one coherent sentence. You will have to delete and rearrange words.

1. The supervisor scheduled a staff meeting. He told us the trouble with the work flow. He spoke to us calmly. The difficulties were serious but not impossible.

2. Ours is an era of rapid change. Political and social movements are often on a collision course. We ignore logically developed language. We prefer the language of confrontation.

3. We often put our own interests and feelings first. We ignore those of the reader. We are inconsiderate. This may affect the tone of our correspondence.

4. Logical fallacies are verbal assaults upon the intelligence of the reader. They are being used every day. They distort rather than clarify reality.

5. Good judgments avoid rigid classifications. People especially should not be classified. There are unpredictable elements in any inference or judgment.

6. Good paragraphs are the secret to coherence. They should be rightly used. They can effectively organize the phases of thought in a report.

Exercise 6   Chapter Five   COHERENCE OF PARAGRAPHS

Directions: Add transitional words where needed in the following paragraphs to make them coherent.

1. The Government has its own jargon that its employees usually understand, not always. Use of jargon is often unavoidable. If a term can be understood by all employees, its use in a publication is usually acceptable. Many occupational specialties have their own special language. Use of jargon may be unavoidable at times; a special term may be used to describe a function, no other term describes it as well. The use of jargon should be limited as much as possible. People outside the specialty will not understand the special terms.

5-38

Exercise 6--page two

2. Our life is influenced in large measure by commercial advertising. Publicity is undertaken only in the interest of the advertisers not of the consumers. The public has been made to believe that white bread is better than brown. The flour has been sifted more and more thoroughly and deprived of its most nutritious elements. Treatment permits its preservation for longer periods and facilitates the making of bread. The millers and the bakers make more money. The consumers eat an inferior product, believing it to be a superior one.

Exercise 6--page three

3. If this course in Effective Writing is to be of value to me, it must contribute to the efficiency of my office. I will try to relate the techniques to the writing I do. I must consider the experience I have had, the knowledge I have of my duties, and the possible effect of introducing changes too rapidly. If a change in method will contribute to the branch or division activity, I will try to introduce it. I will consider carefully the effect on other people in the organization and will attempt to persuade them to accept the change willingly. I will keep foremost in my mind the <u>purpose</u> of any change --to contribute to the better economy and efficiency of the organization.

Exercise 7　　　　　　　　Chapter Five　　　　　　　　COHERENCE

Directions: In the following sets of sentences arrange the sentences in the best order for good coherence and unity:

A. 1. Some semanticists have referred to this practice as the "right name" fallacy.
   2. While few difficulties occur when scientists classify species of flowers, birds, rocks, etc., enormous injustices may result from trying to classify people and their conduct.
   3. Classifications in science have been, of course, and continue to be, essential in codifying and advancing knowledge.
   4. Thus, most bigotry and prejudice is rooted in this tendency to assign a label to a certain person or group.
   5. One of the cleverest ways to mislead a reader into accepting judgments as facts is to use the device of classification.
   6. We believe too often that if we find a name or pin a label on a person or a subject, we have said all there is to say about the subject.

The topic sentence is number _____; then the other sentences should be arranged as follows: _____.

B. 1. Will we bury ourselves in our own red tape or can we be saved from another Tower of Babel and continuing confusion or our native language?
   2. But, in spite of this training, employees are often expected to read and act upon someone else's vague thoughts, presented in ponderous, impressive diction.
   3. Too many writers specialize in their own jargon, and the bewildered reader is the unwitting victim.
   4. Communications are in danger of bogging down in a jungle of meaningless words.
   5. Too often this results in communication channels becoming clogged with verbiage, and, of course, efficiency is reduced.
   6. Writers are taught in English classes that skill in writing is based upon clarity, conciseness, and effectiveness (in that order of importance).

The topic sentence is number _____; then the other sentences should be arranged as follows: _____.

5-41

Exercise 8　　　　　　　　Chapter Five　　　　　　　　COHERENCE

Directions: Write a coherent paragraph below on any subject. Construct a rough draft first, then revise it for the final paragraph. Finally, underline the topic sentence, and **circle** the **verbal connectives** (use all four types listed in the text on page 5-11).

Rough Draft:

Final Paragraph:

Questions and/or Comments for Class Discussion

GOOD WRITING IS CONSIDERATE

CHAPTER 6

PART TWO

Chapter Six--Good Writing is Considerate

Objectives of Chapter Six:

1. To show the advantage of the YOU attitude.
2. To determine how facts differ from inferences and judgments.
3. To examine the use of intensives and hedgers.
4. To explain the dangers of logical fallacies.
5. To choose positive over negative expressions.
6. To check "relative" words.

The following anonymous quotation contains good advice:

Success in communication depends upon three things:

1. Who says it.
2. What they say.
3. HOW they say it.

and of these three "What they say" is sometimes the <u>least</u> important.

This chapter will mainly consider "How they say it."

A. The <u>YOU</u> <u>Attitude</u>

Up to this point we have concentrated on clarity, conciseness and coherence. These qualities are related more to the content of the message (What they say) than to "Who says it" and "How they say it." Hardly anyone would deny that the success of the message depends in part upon a sincere and considerate attitude between communicators. Many have described this relationship as the YOU attitude.

In the words of one writer:

"Business is spelled first with a <u>U</u> then with an <u>I</u>. The wise writer put YOU first then <u>I</u>."

If you put your own interests and feelings first and ignore those of the reader, an inconsiderate tone may result. But a considerate tone can come about by putting yourself in the reader's place and asking yourself, "How would I feel or react if I received my own correspondence?" Apply the Golden Rule to your writing--Do unto others as you would have them do unto you. This will encourage you to treat the reader as a fellow human being.

Did the author of the following statements use the YOU attitude?

1. Because you failed to understand our policy, we cannot allow a refund.

2. We cannot be expected to take care of your routine request--send your inquiry to our local office.

>ANALYSIS: The first example is an accusation insulting the reader's intelligence. The combination of "you" with the negative word "failed" bristles with ill will. In the second example the writer has almost certainly turned away a potential customer by his abrupt, offensive tone.
>
>REVISIONS (using the YOU attitude):
>
>1. Perhaps there has been a misunderstanding...or perhaps we were not clear about our policy on refunds.
>
>2. Thank you for your request for information about our product line. We have promptly referred it to our local office at 126 North Davis Street in your city. Our manager there will call you early next week....
>
>PRINCIPLE: Think carefully about the purpose of your correspondence. Should you deliberately try to irritate, annoy, or insult your reader? If you do, will he be more or less likely to do what you ask of him?

Remember that words are merely symbols. The attitude that these symbols convey is often more important than the words themselves. Creating and maintaining a good atmosphere between communicators can hardly be overemphasized. This "climate" is crucial in clearing the channels of communication between writer and reader. And the failure to communicate successfully is many times not so much a matter of vocabulary as of emotion.

At this point it would be well to review the material in Chapter One on the key words PURPOSE and ATTITUDE. Have you really held your purpose clearly in mind during the writing process? How do you feel about the business of writing? Your answers to these questions are bound to affect the tone of your communication.

Further, take another look at Chapter Two, especially the data on the three worlds--Real World, Word World, and Idea World (see Figure 1 on page 2-3). Study again the human tendency toward stereotyping, narrowing, and mapping, presented on pages 2-4 and 2-5. You may now see more clearly why the writing must first serve the reader's interests and desires.

Here is a list of action words showing the difference between the YOU and I attitudes:

YOU attitude	I attitude
asks his advice	dictates to him
prepares him for changes	imposes changes without consulting him
considers his feelings	considers only his performance
develops his potential	points out his weaknesses
shows respect	shows authority
shows concern and sympathy	puts him in his place
gets his cooperation	forces him to conform
treats him as a person	treats him as a subordinate
encourages his ideas	imposes ideas on him
praises	insults
trains	requires obedience
educates	requires conformity
helps	hurts
clears up	confuses
informs	propagandizes
explains	threatens

In the list above isn't it evident that the "I" attitude fosters an insincere and condescending view of others? Writers and speakers need to ask themselves if this is the way to accomplish the real _purpose_ of communication. There is a simple and practical reason for using the YOU attitude--readers are more likely to respond to a courteous and logical approach; they will naturally resist a discourteous and arrogant one. It's just good business sense to state our ideas forthrightly, courteously, and honestly, for this is the _only_ way to convince others of our views or to get them to do what we want. The YOU attitude, then, asks us to keep the reader's interests clearly in mind, and, as communicators, to set aside our own concerns.

B. Facts--Inferences--Judgments

A very important part of being considerate of the reader involves how we present our ideas. The "ethics" of the writer-reader relationship requires us to be as fair and impartial as possible in our communications. But in our era of rapid change with its almost head-on collision of political and social movements, there has often been an ignoring of logically developed language in favor of the language of confrontation. Extremist groups purposely set about to convince us not by reason but by inflammatory rhetoric. Advertisers chant the praises of their products with flagrant disregard for the truth. Politicians' speeches are often designed not to explain their positions but to make us mad enough at their opponents to solicit votes. Being immersed in a sea of inflated, and often downright deceptive, rhetoric cannot help having an effect upon us. We sometimes mistakenly choose our words for the effect they will create rather than for the reality they should reflect.

A great advocate of clear, simple English, Jonathan Swift, writing in the 1700's, often pointed to "affected" language as an obstacle to considerate writer-reader relationhips. Here is an excerpt from his essay "Proper Words in Proper Places":

> Although, as I have already observed, our English tongue is too little cultivated in this kingdom, yet the faults are nine in ten owing to affectation, not to the want of understanding. When a man's thoughts are clear, the properest words will generally offer themselves first, and his own judgment will direct him in what order to place them, so as they may be best understood. When men err against this method, it is usually on purpose, and to show their learning, their oratory, their politeness, or their knowledge of the world. In short, that simplicity without which no human performance can arrive to any great perfection, is nowhere more eminently useful than in this....

Now let us consider in detail the important distinctions among FACTS, INFERENCES and JUDGMENTS. In order to make these differences clear to the reader, the writer must, of course, first recognize them himself, then present them correctly in his writing. Here are the basic definitions:

1. _Facts_ are verifiable; they are statements referring to truths that can be checked, either by personal observation or by referring to a trustworthy authority.

EXAMPLE: The distance from Davenport, Iowa, to St. Paul, Minnesota, is 332 miles by the shortest route from one city limit to the other.

2. _Inferences_ are statements made about the unknown on the basis of the known. While there are factual bases for the inference, it goes beyond the facts and brings something not completely verifiable into the statement.

EXAMPLE: The Soviet delegate scowled at the ambassador, shouted loudly, took off his shoes, and pounded them on the table. He was furious at the American delegation. (Note that the writer is making an inference by saying "He was furious, etc." While probably acceptable, it is nonetheless an inference presented as fact.

3. <u>Judgments.</u> While all judgments record the speaker's or writer's approval or disapproval of something, some are more acceptable than others. Of course, there is no such thing as a perfect opinion, for even more than inferences, judgments contain elements of the unknown.

To evaluate the usefulness of a judgment, try to test its validity. Double check to be sure that the judgment is based on reliable and qualified data. The following checklist can be used to assess the validity of judgments:

1. <u>Reliable</u> -- Is your informant an expert in the field? Is he a trustworthy individual, both personally and professionally? Is he an excitable type likely to make snap judgments? Does he have a personal interest or prejudice that could affect his opinions? For example, could a supervisor be entirely objective about a proposal to reduce his work force by half?

2. <u>Qualified</u> -- Consider your informant's credentials. How much experience has he had? At what level? Are his education and training sufficient to make his opinions valid? For example, whose view of a change in hiring policies would be more acceptable--the Personnel Manager's or the Assistant Accountant's?

In using support material be careful to distinguish between the following types of opinion:

<u>Value Judgments.</u> An opinion from a reliable and qualified informant becomes a value judgment. But even when one source appears reliable and qualified, it is wise to consider possible conflicting views. For instance, this statement: "I believe that the product is acceptable because five of the quality control experts agree" might be questioned if three equally qualified experts disagree. The writer should at least mention this disagreement in his report.

Personal Judgments. On the other hand, if an opinion seems unsupported, it may be just a personal judgment. Watch how your sources state their opinions. If they use such phrases as these: "I just have a gut feeling that ...," "I have a hunch that ...," "I would guess that ...," ask them to cite better reasons. Intuition alone is not a valid basis for action.

In the following example and its revision notice the difference between a judgmental and a factual approach:

EXAMPLE: The supervisor has been stubborn, deceitful, and unfair in his treatment of my request for a transfer in job assignment. (The statement is highly emotional and suggests a history of ill will between employee and supervisor. Such a personal judgment needs factual support to be convincing.)

REVISION: The supervisor has not responded to my request for a job transfer made over six months ago. He informed the Division Head in a memo dated 11/15/83 that my request had been denied, but I have had no official notice of his decision. My concern and uncertainty about this matter are affecting my job performance. May I have an answer soon?

COMMENT: Upon further investigation, the reader may come to the same conclusion as the writer--that the supervisor is stubborn, deceitful, and unfair. But the revision presents the complaint in a rational and factual way. This will prove far more persuasive than resorting to "name-calling" tactics.

Of course, inferences and judgments have an important and necessary place in report writing. The progress and success of an organization often depends upon employees making sound inferences and judgments. Without them changes would be impossible. What is very important, however, is to word your writing with care in order to label such statements clearly. Reports that do not distinguish between fact and opinion are very unreliable instruments.

The following methods are useful in labeling inferences and judgments:

1. Use conditional verb forms.

    EXAMPLE:

    The project | could be / may be / should be / might be | completed on schedule.

6-6

2. Use conditional "if" clauses.

   EXAMPLE:

If conditions remain constant,	**the project will**
If funds are available,	**be completed**
If added personnel are assigned,	**on schedule.**
If the material is suitable,	

3. Use expressions within the sentence, such as:

shows a trend toward	based on what we now know
can be expected to	perhaps it will happen
shows every indication now	probably it does show
is moving toward	the data point toward
we infer from this	our judgment is that

If the reader mis-reads inferences and judgments as facts and ACTS upon them as facts, irreparable harm can be done. Qualifiers like the ones above are helpful signals leading the reader to interpret your material correctly.

C. <u>Watch</u> <u>the</u> <u>Use</u> <u>of</u> <u>Intensives</u> <u>and</u> <u>Hedgers</u>

A statement like this: "It was a wonderful and very valuable conference." presents an unsupported judgment. Better writing practice would cite first the factual and practical information received at the conference; then by way of summary could refer to it as a valuable and inspiring experience. Give the reader the facts first--then your judgment may be acceptable.

Writers trying to impress readers often use intensives like these: <u>great</u>, <u>marvelous</u>, <u>stupendous</u>, <u>mind-boggling</u>, <u>exceptional</u>, <u>tremendous</u>, <u>colossal</u>, <u>gigantic</u>, etc.

   EXAMPLE:

   <u>Not this</u>--The Personnel Director courageously stood by his principles by voting against the proposal.

   <u>Say this</u>--The Personnel Director cast the only vote against the proposal.

   COMMENT: The first statement injects your own judgment of the Director's action into the account. The second sticks to the facts.

Also the considerate writer avoids hedging or "weasel-wording." A hedger tries to create escape routes for himself to cover up his uncertainty about or unwillingness to take a position.

EXAMPLES:

1. <u>Normally</u>, we can grant a request such as yours. But yours is unusual. (The first sentence misleads the reader, the second is patronizing in tone.)

2. Your quarterly report <u>seems to</u> reflect a downward trend in sales. ("Seems" weakens the statement.)

3. <u>Ordinarily</u>, in cases like this, the employee is given a second chance. But this case <u>seems</u> to merit dismissal. (<u>Ordinarily</u> and <u>seems</u> weaken the sentence and mislead the reader.)

Be careful of these "hedgers" unless you have a real reason for using them:

Apparently	As a rule	Normally
It appears	In most cases	Ordinarily
Seemingly	In many instances	As a usual case
Usually	Seems to indicate	In general
Generally	Commonly	Basically

D. Avoid <u>Logical</u> <u>Fallacies</u>

Logical fallacies are verbal assaults upon the intelligence of the reader. An unethical writer can use them to purposely distort rather than to clarify an issue. Fallacies cleverly manipulate language on the verbal level but lead to unsupported or false conclusions. Writers should be able to recognize these traps of logic in other's writing and avoid them in their own. The following list explains some of the more common types of fallacies:

1. <u>Hasty</u> or broad <u>generalizations</u>--These involve a conclusion based upon insufficient or inconclusive evidence.

    EXAMPLE: My experience with several training courses in effective writing at this installation over the past two years proves the success of this type of training.

    COMMENT: Certainly a wider survey than your own experience would be needed to prove this conclusion.

2. <u>Transfer</u> <u>device</u> (<u>ad</u> <u>verecundiam</u>)--Here the statement attempts to transfer prestige, value, or glory (or oppositely the shame and disgrace) from one thing or person to another.

EXAMPLES: Franklin Roosevelt would thoroughly disapprove of these cutbacks in Social Security.
"Watergate" tactics like these show how corrupt my opponent really is.

COMMENT: The first statement tries to capitalize on the reputation of Roosevelt, and there is no way of soliciting his opinion. The second statement seeks to discredit the opposing candidate by the "Watergate" reference.

3. *Argument to the people (the bandwagon approach)*--Here the appeal is for the reader to go along with the crowd--everybody else is doing it, why not you?

EXAMPLE: Over sixty companies in your area are using Ditto Copiers. Why not join them?

COMMENT: The argument from numbers alone is not convincing. A logically directed argument would point out how this copier could bring economy and efficiency to the operation.

4. *Faulty connection between cause and effect (post hoc, ergo propter hoc)*--"After this, therefore because of this."

EXAMPLE: All I know is that we didn't have an absentee problem until after he became the supervisor.

COMMENT: This fallacy tries to equate cause and effect with simple chronology--because something happens before something else, the first is the cause of the second. Other possible contributing factors are ignored. In the example above higher absenteeism could have been caused by other factors: weather, epidemics of illness, poorer working conditions, etc.

5. *Non-sequitur (it does not follow)*--This faulty thinking results from making an inference not justified by the data from which it is drawn.

EXAMPLE: Since Spain has been a dictatorship for many years, recent Spanish immigrants will not make good American citizens.

COMMENT: The statement assumes that life under a totalitarian regime is an obstacle to a later life in a democratic system. In fact, the opposite argument could be advanced--such immigrants might make very good citizens because they would better appreciate a free society than native Americans.

6. **Begging the question**--also called "arguing in a circle," for it assumes the truth of what the writer is trying to prove.

   EXAMPLE: Creative writing is more difficult than report writing because it is harder to do successfully.

   COMMENT: Here the writer uses "difficult" in the first part of the sentence, meaning essentially the same as "harder to do" in the second clause.

7. **Illogical Comparisons.**

   a. The "agency" comparative--the term is derived from advertising agencies' over-use of words like **better**, **faster**, **cleaner**, etc. with no second term to compare with the first.

   EXAMPLE: Weedos have **lower** tar and nicotine content. They are a **better** cigarette.

   COMMENT: To what other cigarettes are Weedos being compared? Correct use of the comparative terms **lower** and **better** requires another item for comparison.

   b. Illogical position of comparative terms--this results from incorrect placement of the comparative phrase.

   EXAMPLE: Weedos are as good as, if not better than, all other brands of cigarettes.

   REVISION: Weedos are as good as all other brands of cigarettes, if not better.

   COMMENT: The logical position for the qualifying "if" phrase is at the end of the sentence. That is, make the full comparison first, then add the qualifier.

8. **Argument to the man** (ad hominem)--This fallacy attempts to divert attention away from real issues by attacking one's opponent on a personal basis.

   EXAMPLE: How could he function successfully as a supervisor? He's had a lot of problems with his family, you know.

   COMMENT: The statements falsely assume that personal difficulties would interfere with job performance. Sometimes, of course, one's private and public life have a bearing on each other, but no evidence for this is cited in the example.

9. __The either ... or fallacy__. This is also called the "false alternative." Here the writer assumes that a question can be approached in only two ways--one good and one bad, or both bad. This fallacy ignores the possibility of other options in solving a serious or complicated problem.

> EXAMPLES: City politicians are either unqualified or corrupt.
>
> We must either reduce taxes or see more and more people sink to the poverty level.
>
> COMMENT: These statements simplify complex issues in an attempt to make the writer's position seem convincing. Are __all__ politicians unqualified or corrupt? Are there other alternatives to prevent poverty?

E. __Choose positive over negative expression whenever possible__. It makes good sense to use words with favorable rather than unfavorable connotations. Words do have personalities (good or bad) just as people do. They can suggest pleasant or unpleasant attitudes. For example, one person might describe a refrigerator as "half-full" another as "half-empty." A weather forecast could refer to "partly sunny" or "partly cloudy" skies. A letter answering a customer complaint might be mistakenly phrased this way:

> Please accept our belated apology for the failure of our equipment and the dissatisfaction you had as a result of this unfortunate error. Our local office will arrange to replace the defective machine.

The seven gloomy words used would probably remind the customer all over again of his bad experience. Getting rid of most of the negative words turns it into a positive message:

> We are sorry for the trouble you have had. A new machine is being shipped today. Our local office will call you Monday morning to arrange for installation.

While as writers we cannot be expected to express "sweetness and light" at all times, we can check our writing by asking:

> Could I change that around to more positive expression and still get the same meaning?

A New York Life Insurance Company study of reader attitudes revealed the following:

MOST PEOPLE LIKE THESE WORDS

ability	courtesy	grateful	notable	service
abundant	definite	guarantee	opportunity	simplicity
achieve	dependable	handsome	perfection	sincerity
active	deserving	harmonious	permanent	stability
admirable	desirable	helpful	perseverance	substantial
advance	determined	honesty	pleasant	success
advantage	distinction	honor	popularity	superior
ambition	diversity	humor	practical	supremacy
appreciate	ease	imagination	praiseworthy	thorough
approval	economy	improvement	prestige	thought
aspire	effective	industry	proficient	thoughtful
attainment	efficient	ingenuity	progress	thrift
authoritative	energy	initiative	prominent	truth
benefit	enhance	integrity	propriety	valuable
capable	enthusiasm	intelligence	punctual	vigor
cheer	equality	judgment	reasonable	vital
comfort	excellence	justice	recognition	vivid
commendable	exceptional	kind	recommend	wisdom
commendation	exclusive	lasting	reliable	
comprehensive	expedite	liberal	reputable	

Now look over the above list of words again. Do you recognize many of these words as favorites in product advertising? Advertisers would be far less likely to choose the words in the following list.

MOST PEOPLE DISLIKE THESE WORDS

abandoned	deadlock	ignorant	obstinate	standstill
abuse	decline	ignoble	opinionated	struggling
alibi	disaster	illiterate	oversight	stunted
apology	discredit	imitation	precipitate	tamper
bankrupt	dispute	immature	prejudiced	tardy
beware	evict	implicate	premature	timid
biased	exaggerate	impossible	pretentious	tolerable
blame	fail	improvident	retrench	unfair
calamity	failure	insolvent	rude	unfortunate
careless	fault	in vain	ruin	unsuccessful
cheap	fear	liable	shirk	untimely
collapse	flagrant	long-winded	shrink	waste
collusion	flat	meager	sketchy	weak
commonplace	flimsy	mediocre	slack	worry
complaint	fraud	misfortune	smattering	wrong
crisis	hardship	neglect	squander	
crooked	hazy	negligence	stagnant	

6-12

F. **Watch the use of "relative" words.** A relative word, usually a modifier, has an unstable, flexible quality. Because of differences in background and training, the writer and the reader may not understand the word in the same way.

> EXAMPLES (Without added explanation, wouldn't the underlined words in the following sentences be a possible source of confusion?):
>
> Write a <u>brief</u> report on Project X. Prepare a <u>thorough</u> briefing on Plan B. The survey was a <u>difficult</u> assignment. Give the bucket a <u>light</u> tap with the hammer.

The last example above was once used by a foreman as an order to a big, muscular laborer. He interpreted the "light tap" quite differently than the foreman intended and gave the bucket a hefty blow, splitting it wide open!

<u>Summary</u>

Being considerate of your reader involves using the YOU attitude; distinguishing facts from inferences and judgments; watching your use of intensives, hedgers, and relative words; avoiding logical fallacies; and using positive expression. Finally, the following checklist may be helpful:

1. Does your writing have a truly human tone without being condescending or patronizing?
2. Does your wording clearly make distinctions among facts, inferences, and judgments?
3. Are the sources for your data both reliable and qualified?
4. Have you checked your writing for objectivity and avoided inflated or emotional statements?
5. Have you checked the completeness and accuracy of your information, keeping your reading audience in mind?
6. Have you, as much as possible, used a positive rather than a negative approach?

Exercise 1   Chapter Six   "YOU" ATTITUDE

Directions: In the following sentences change the wording to reflect the YOU attitude:

1. We are sorry when anybody is not completely satisfied.

2. We have your letter in which you claim that the clock was received in a damaged condition.

3. Contrary to your opinion the bill became due and payable on the 15th of the month.

4. In your last order you failed to list any catalog numbers.

5. You are hereby notified that we cannot be held responsible for your negligence.

6. You must be altogether ignorant of our procedures.

7. You would have had to be aware that there was an error in your last order.

Exercise 1--page two

8. Obviously, you do not have nearly enough working capital to consider our offer.

9. We have indeed tried to consider your feelings in this matter, a fact you do not seem to recognize.

10. I suppose we will have to make good the alleged shortage in your shipment.

11. You forgot to list your references on the form enclosed.

12. We can't do anything about your request until you furnish complete information.

13. We will appreciate it if you honor this invoice without any further delay or argument.

14. Please send us the name of a good lawyer in your town. We may have to sue you.

15. You know that you should always send any inquiries to the home office.

Exercise 2   Chapter Six   "YOU" ATTITUDE

Directions: Revise this letter from an insurance company to improve the tone:

   Please be kind enough to fill in the requested data completely this time. We have been patient about this, and we are trying to help you recover the cost of the damages you claim you received from the accident you had with one of our policy holders. This is the second time we have had to write to you about this. You <u>must</u> put on the form enclosed the same information provided on the original accident report. Then we will see what we can do for you. A company the size of ours insists upon complete information on our own forms, particularly when the claim is as small as yours. Observe further that we must have your responses in ink, witnessed by two reliable people and notarized. We have provided you with a postage-free envelope.

   We sincerely want to cooperate with you on this matter.

                                        Cordially yours,

Exercise 3   Chapter Six   FACTS-INFERENCES-JUDGMENTS

Directions: Write one of the following terms after each sentence: fact, inference, value judgment, or personal judgment. If you choose inference or judgment, write "acceptable" or "unacceptable" after each.

1. Stock prices rose sixteen points yesterday.

2. Our profits, based on the leading trend indicators, should rise by 10% during the next year.

3. Astrological influences have a great deal to do with one's success or failure in business.

4. The will to succeed and the ability to do so are necessary ingredients in financial success.

5. In the reorganization three positions will be eliminated.

6. In the reorganization three positions were eliminated.

7. The salesman claimed that the X computer would solve all of our accounting problems.

8. There is something fishy about the whole scheme; therefore, I'll vote against it.

9. The Personnel Manager never hires redheads because he says they always go through doorways first.

10. I just have an inner feeling that the new program won't work, call it intuition if you like!

Exercise 3--page two

11. Based on wholesale price adjustments we can expect a drop in retail prices during the next six months.

12. Improvement in your writing skills is assured by completing this course.

13. You will learn new techniques for improving your writing skills by successfully completing this course.

14. Evidence of completion of this course will be recorded in your official transcript.

15. The Quality Control supervisor believes that we should purchase a better grade of steel to avoid rejects.

16. The Chief Accountant is opposed to changing the factory work flow on the basis of the latest time study.

17. A total of 242 students were enrolled in Effective Writing last year.

18. The training supervisor favors offering more courses in written communication during next year.

19. The prisoner cooperated with the prosecutor by revealing his cellmate's confession of guilt.

20. The company president stated only that he had a strong feeling against marketing the product now.

Exercise 4   Chapter Six   LOGICAL FALLACIES

Directions: Write after each sentence the number of one of the following fallacies to identify the illogic in the sentence:

1. Hasty generalization (insufficient evidence)
2. Transfer device (conveys value or disgrace from one thing to another)
3. Argument to the people ("join the crowd")
4. Faulty cause and effect relationship ("<u>after</u> this, therefore, <u>because</u> of this")
5. Non-sequitur (an inference not justified by data)
6. Begging the question (assumes the truth of what it's trying to prove)
7. Illogical comparison (no second term to compare with the first)
8. Illogical comparison ("if" clauses in the wrong place in the sentence)
9. Argument to the man (attack on a personal basis)
10. The either...or fallacy (presenting only two alternatives)

1. Five different companies in our area have adopted the employee profit-sharing plan; therefore, we should adopt it immediately. _____

2. You can bet Henry Ford would never have tolerated such coddling of employees as we put up with today. _____

3. Most democracies have experienced the gradual erosion of individual freedoms: ours will go the same direction. _____

4. Most problems of bad morale in an organization occur because employees lack good will toward their fellow workers and management. _____

5. We must perform in a better way to remain competitive and earn greater profits. _____

6. The corrosion with aluminum is as bad as, if not worse than, with the steel parts. _____

7. The change in top management obviously brought about the subsequent decline in production. _____

8. He'll never get results from his sales force with those Gestapo tactics. _____

Exercise 4--page two

9. What does he know about the responsibility of running a business? He never met a payroll in his life? _____

10. He operated like a dictator twice before when he was promoted to managerial posts, so we can expect the same this time. _____

11. If Thomas Jefferson were alive today, he would devote his full energies to enacting all plans in our party platform. _____

12. The number of airplane accidents proves that air travel is unsafe. _____

13. I prefer the X computer because it is my choice of the best record-keeping equipment. _____

14. This machine has far greater possibilities and will give you much less trouble. _____

15. Our candidate was born in a log cabin, was self-educated, and has always supported the poor and underprivileged. _____

16. There is something about the look in those cold eyes of his that tells me he is ruthless. _____

17. Jones wouldn't be a good choice for the position--remember that trouble he had with his wife last year. _____

18. These stocks are a good investment--they have declined somewhat in the last six months, but when they are low is a good time to buy. _____

19. If you're not part of the solution, you're part of the problem. _____

20. Power corrupts; and absolute power corrupts absolutely. _____

21. He is not a decisive person because he is unable to make proper judgments at the proper time. _____

22. Life is either a great adventure or it is nothing. _____

23. Jazz is more complex than rock music because it is harder to play. _____

Exercise 5 Chapter Six

INTENSIVES
HEDGERS
RELATIVE WORDS

Directions: In the following sentences draw a line through the intensives and hedgers. Circle any relative words.

1. The over-all program for improving ~~long~~ reports in this office has been ~~basically~~ successful.

2. ~~Deepest~~ regret is felt by ~~nearly~~ everyone that your ~~superb~~ suggestion cannot be utilized at this time.

3. ~~Generally~~ the inspector made a routine inspection, but, ~~brief~~ as it was, it brought to light the ~~most amazing~~ revelations.

4. ~~Undoubtedly~~ you will find this ~~thorough~~ guide of ~~unparalleled~~ benefit to all students of writing.

5. After an ~~apparently most~~ painstaking search of the back files, Jones presented a ~~very astute and perceptive~~ analysis of our ~~serious~~ problem.

6. In your briefing give us a ~~basically short~~ analysis of the history of the project, then devote more time to our expectations of its ~~promising~~ future.

7. ~~Ordinarily~~ use a thicker mold for the initial tool-and-die operation; then be ~~extremely~~ careful in removing the casting.

Exercise 5--page two

8. The speaker seemed to use the most tactless and boorish behavior which completely disenchanted the large audience.

9. Our sales have made seemingly gigantic strides under the superb leadership of our most able manager.

10. His secretary was generally a little on the thin side, but with his colossal size they made an apparently amazing contrast.

Questions and/or Comments for Class Discussion

GOOD WRITING IS CORRECT

CHAPTER 7

PART TWO

Chapter Seven--Good Writing is Correct

Objectives of Chapter Seven:

1. To examine how usage affects language change.
2. To point out eight common usage problems and ways to correct them.

Ours is an age of rapid change affecting almost every aspect of our lives. New technological developments and social movements have revolutionized our ways of thinking and acting. Since standards and values are being re-examined, many people like to depend on the security offered by traditional language labels. Take politics, for example. In an attempt to understand their positions more clearly we still prefer to classify candidates and officeholders according to the old names <u>liberal</u> and <u>conservative</u>. But just ask any office-seeker or incumbent whether he is a liberal or a conservative and get ready for an incredible amount of verbiage disclaiming either label.

Such labels become fuzzy in meaning because language is always a bit old-fashioned. A so-called "cultural lag" exists between social and political changes and the words used to describe them. The dictionary makers try to catch up with current usage but never quite do.

We use the slightly dated words <u>liberal</u> and <u>conservative</u> as well in the field of grammar and language use. But, like politics, the terms, strictly applied, mark such extreme and unreal positions that few can be found in either camp. Those few, however, are often a very vocal minority! A strict conservative (purist or proscriptive grammarian are more usual terms) opposes almost any language change while a liberal is willing to accept almost any new usage. In making practical judgments on correct and acceptable use of the language, however, we find the terms <u>purist</u> and <u>conservative</u> difficult to apply. The forces for change in the language are constantly at work. And when a <u>majority</u> of the educated users of English accept a new usage, it becomes a reputable part of the language. Our judgments about acceptability in language use might again be guided by the wisdom of Alexander Pope who wrote:

> Be not the first by whom the new are tried,
> Nor yet the last to lay the old aside.

This textbook does not attempt a complete treatment of the rules of grammar and usage. Mechanics are adequately presented in hundreds of texts on the market today--some lean toward the purist, some toward the liberal side. Rather our effort in this chapter on correctness will be to isolate and study areas of major trouble for modern writers. We will also become aware of some practical "short-cut" methods, leading to correct usage. Adding the fifth "C"--CORRECTNESS--will complete the recipe for successful writing.

A. <u>Is Some Modern Fiction Ungrammatical?</u>

First of all, how can many modern writers of fiction ignore many of the rules of grammar? Can we criticize such fine writers as Saul Bellow, Philip Roth, and John Updike as lacking knowledge of correctness? William Strunk, Jr. in his <u>Elements of Style</u> answers the question this way:

> It is an old observation that the best writers sometimes disregard the rules of rhetoric. When they do so, however, the reader will usually find in the sentence some compensating merit, attained at the cost of the violation. Unless he [the writer] is certain of doing as well, he will probably do best to follow the rules.

After all, literature, as an art form, may depart from the ordinary rules to create artistic effects. Sometimes the artist departs from reality altogether in his attempt to free himself from the sensory and the earthly. Abstract art, for example, leads us to an existence not available to the ordinary perceptions of our senses. But since we do not often use literary English in government and business, observance of the rules of grammar will best assure clear and acceptable writing.

B. <u>What About the Purist View?</u>

Some well-meaning writers, however, become over-fastidious about applying the rules of grammar. Perhaps the strict training they received in grade and high school English classes continues to influence their language habits. But some of these "unbreakable" rules have been relaxed in modern English. Check yourself on the following sentences. Would you accept these usages?

1. The boss said that this was a problem he would not put up with.
2. If I was the supervisor, I would make some changes around here.
3. I wish to sincerely thank you for your cooperation on this.

4. My job is not as well defined as yours.
5. Try and arrive on time for the meeting.
6. I will consult with you about the report at tomorrow's meeting.
7. But the opposition to the change was strong.

You may have been taught differently, but all except possibly one of these sentences (number 5) would be considered correct usage today. The first sentence, for example, contains a preposition at the end of the sentence. Here is Churchill's often-quoted reply to an officious proof-reader who had "corrected" Sir Winston's sentences by carefully tucking all the prepositions within the sentences: "This is the kind of arrant nonsense up with which I will not put."

Or perhaps the classic sentence, illustrating just how flexible our language is, comes in the complaint of a small boy to his father just at bedtime: "Why did you bring that book that I didn't want to be read to out of up for?" Count them! There are five prepositions at the end of the sentence, yet the thought comes through in spite of the odd rhetoric.

Some old usages refuse to die a decent death and have survived with surprising strength. For example, most language experts have decided that the old objection to using the word "contact" as a verb has disappeared. Yet a recent dictionary for the use of technical writers criticizes the sentence: "I will contact you as soon as possible." The author frowns on the use of contact as a verb and suggests substitutes such as inform, get in touch, advise, let you know, etc.

Would you consider the following sentences correct?

1. And she is exceeding wise.
2. This was the most unkindest cut of all.
3. I have broke with her father.
4. I will...yet give me no thousand crowns neither.
5. All debts are cleared between you and I.
6. Each was leaning on their elbows.
7. Don Pedro is returned to seek you.

All the preceding are quotations from the plays of Shakespeare and were correct usage in the Sixteenth Century. Obviously, four hundred years of history have greatly changed the standards of correctness.

PRINCIPLE: The best advice to be given to modern writers is to avoid these extremes:
1. The purist view because it often makes language stilted and old-fashioned in style.
2. The liberal view because unfamiliar usages will at best irritate the reader and at worst bewilder him.

Don't be either a stuffed shirt or a grammatical "hippie" in your use of language!

C. <u>Levels</u> <u>of</u> <u>Usage</u> <u>for</u> <u>Written</u> <u>English</u>

In some respects we cannot really talk about correctness in the abstract. We should ask "Correct for whom?" because the situation and the audience must be considered. What is appropriate and correct for one group or on one occasion may be ineffective for another. The chart below attempts to suggest typical uses of English on the various levels:

<u>Standard Usage</u>

Formal English (spoken or written)

<u>Typical</u> <u>Uses</u>--oratory, eulogies, graduation addresses, merit citations, books and articles written for technically oriented or well-educated audiences.

<u>Typical</u> <u>Qualities</u>--scholarly vocabulary, lengthy sentences, figurative language, literary allusions, may stress rhythm and sound patterns in sentences and paragraphs, abstract terms.

General English (spoken and written)

<u>Typical</u> <u>Uses</u>--business correspondence, articles in "digest" magazines, newspaper stories, texts for secondary school students.

<u>Typical</u> <u>Qualities</u>--uses more concrete than abstract terms; tries to create clear images in reader's mind; follows patterns of speech more closely than Formal English; avoids contractions, lengthy sentences, and academic-sounding words.

Informal English (more often used in speaking than in writing)

<u>Typical Uses</u>--between writers who know each other personally, in magazines for special groups (auto repairers, rock music fans, wrestlers), in ordinary conversation.

<u>Typical Qualities</u>--allows use of contractions, slang, and shop-talk; sentences and paragraph structure tend to be loose and rambling; stays very close to the patterns of speech.

Sub-standard Usage

Vulgate English   (mainly spoken)

<u>Typical Uses</u>--in speech of uneducated persons, in literary works to record sub-standard speech of characters (legitimate use), dialect and regional expressions, profanity.

<u>Typical Qualities</u>--violates rules of grammar, spelling and pronunciation (see examples in Section D below), uses forms from sub-standard speech, such as <u>et</u> (for <u>ate</u>), <u>youse</u> (for <u>you</u>), <u>drownded</u> (for <u>drowned</u>).

D. <u>Does Your Bad Grammar Show</u>?

The great amount of bad grammar we hear spoken today is evidence enough that many need a brush-up on mechanics. For some the inability to command correct English has held back advancement and resulted in lost opportunities. Sadly enough, most users of incorrect forms in speaking are unaware of their mistakes. We could help each other in this regard, if we were willing to point out (privately and courteously, of course) errors in grammar to others and be willing to accept such advice ourselves without being offended.

Would you want an oral or written presentation from anyone who uses English like this?

1. I done a real good job on this here report.
2. I done told ya ya shouldn't have ought to of done it.
3. Beings as our policies is under fire, we have did the following:
4. Youse shouldn't ought to forget you're facts.

These are serious lapses in correct English--any one of them could be fatal to an employee's chances for advancement.

E. Common Usage Problems

Most writers have difficulty with only a few rules of grammar and punctuation. The following questions identify eight troublesome areas:

1. Does your sentence go far enough (fragment) or too far (run-on sentence)?
2. Are you right on time in your sentence? (tenses of the verb)
3. Are you a good match-maker in your sentences? (consistent subject and verb forms)
4. Whom do you want? (pronoun problems)
5. Have you forgotten the apostrophe? (the most elusive mark)
6. Are you real (or really) confident about your English? (adjective and adverb forms)
7. How about your signals? (punctuation)
8. How is your spelling?

Now let us take up these problem areas one by one.

1. Does your sentence go far enough or too far?

   a. Two identifiable elements must be present in each statement to qualify it as a sentence--actor or agent (subject) and the action (verb). If one of these is missing, the reader may lack something essential for clear understanding--the statement doesn't go far enough. We label this fault as a "fragment."

   EXAMPLES:

   (1) Wonder where the meeting will be held. (no actor)
   (2) Referring to your letter of 16 August. (no actor)
   (3) A meeting that was very valuable. (no actor-no main action)

   NOTE: A major offender here is the "ing" word used toward the beginning of a sentence. In the second sentence above no one is mentioned as the actor in the statement. It should read:

   Referring to your letter of 16 August, we are shipping your order by special delivery.
   OR
   I refer to your order of 16 August.

b. If the statement <u>goes too far</u>, the reader will have trouble separating the run-together ideas in the sentence. This type is called a "run-on" sentence.

EXAMPLES:

(1) Smith looked annoyed the report was not on his desk.
(2) The bid seems reasonable but definite contracts will be necessary.
(3) Your bids look all right however the Board will have to approve it.

These three sentences need separation as follows:

(1) Smith looked annoyed; the report was not on his desk.
(2) The bid seems reasonable, but definite contracts will be necessary.
(3) Your bid looks all right; however, the Board will have to approve it.

c. Special care is required when composing a DOUBLE (compound) SENTENCE, as indicated by the three examples above. To be correct the ideas must be separated according to these definite rules:

(1) If the connective word is one of these: <u>and</u>, <u>but</u>, <u>or</u>, <u>nor</u>, <u>for</u>, <u>so</u>, use a comma in front of it. (See second corrected sentence under b. above.) Incidentally, these six words form a <u>complete</u> list of this type of connective.
(2) If the connective word is one like these: <u>however</u>, <u>nevertheless</u>, <u>therefore</u>, <u>in spite of</u>, <u>then</u>, etc., use a semicolon in front of it and comma after it. (See third corrected sentence under b. above.) These connectives are also adverbs, and there are many more words like them in the language.
(3) If there is no connective (see first corrected sentence under b. above), a semicolon must be used.

2. <u>Are you right on "time"</u> in your sentences? The time referred to by the action (verb) in your sentence is called <u>tense</u>. The six tenses and their forms of expression are listed below:

Primary Tenses

Present   I write
(action going on)   I am writing (progressive)
                       I do write (emphatic)

Past   I wrote
(action finished)   I was writing (progressive)
                       I did write (emphatic)

Future   I will write
(action to come)   I will be writing (progressive)
                       I shall be writing (emphatic)*
                       I am going to write (idiom)

Secondary Tenses

Present Perfect   I have written
(action begun in past, I have been writing (progressive)
may still be going on)

Past Perfect   I had written
(action two steps   I had been writing (progressive)
back of present)

Future Perfect   I will have written
(action occurs between I will have been writing (progressive)
present and future)   I shall have written (emphatic)*

* In American use of English the distinctions in ordinary usage of shall and will are practically gone. But we still use shall to gain strength and emphasis in stating regulations or rules like these: The members shall pay their dues once a year. The employees shall report for work promptly.

    a. "ing" forms (am writing, was writing, have been writing, etc.) are called progressive because they refer to an on-going action or to one that was interrupted.

    EXAMPLES:

    I am writing the report during this week.
    I was writing the report when the supervisor put me on another assignment.

b. The "time line" below helps to illustrate the relationship of the tenses:

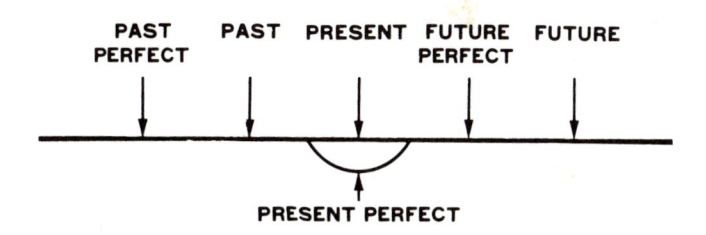

```
    PAST      PAST   PRESENT  FUTURE    FUTURE
   PERFECT                    PERFECT
      |        |        |        |        |
      ↓        ↓        ↓        ↓        ↓
  ────────────────────────────────────────────
                   ↑
            PRESENT PERFECT
```

Figure 14

c. The Present Perfect tense, you will notice, spans the past, present, and into the future. It refers to action repeated on a number of occasions, not yet finished, and likely to occur in a future.

> EXAMPLE: Yes, I have written the reports in this office for the past ten years. (Or the progressive form "have been writing" could be used to add a sense of continuing action.)

d. The Past Perfect is used to refer to an action already completed before another past action.

> EXAMPLE: Before the supervisor called me yesterday, I had written the report.

e. The Future Perfect action on the time line occurs, you will note, between the present and the future. The action is completed even before it has started.

> EXAMPLE: By noon tomorrow I will have written the report.

f. Keep your time relationships consistent in the sentence. If the first part of a sentence refers to a past action, the second verb must use the past tense or a <u>have</u> or <u>had</u> form. Within paragraphs, if you begin with present or past tense, keep the rest of the sentences consistent with the first.

EXAMPLES:

WRONG: He had promised that he will write the report.

Before I asked him, he promised that he will cooperate.

He said at the staff meeting that he forgot his briefcase.

RIGHT: He promised that he would write the report.

Before I asked him, he had promised that he would cooperate.

He said at the staff meeting that he had forgotten his briefcase.

3. <u>Are you a good match-maker in your sentence?</u> This simply refers to consistency between the number (singular or plural) of the subject and the verb. A singular subject (marked "S" below) matches with a singular verb, a plural subject (marked "P" below) with a plural verb.

EXAMPLES:

a. The supervisor refers to that policy.
       S   S

The supervisors refer to that policy.
     P   P

b. The supervisor and his assistant agree on the policy.
     S   +   S = P

RULE: Two subjects joined by <u>and</u> add up to a plural.

c. The supervisor <u>or</u> his assistant agrees on the policy.
     S   or   S = S

RULE: Two singular subjects joined by <u>or</u> take a singular verb. They do <u>not</u> add up.

d. The supervisor or his assistants agree on the policy.
     S   or   P = P

RULE: When one singular and one plural subject are joined by or, the verb matches with the nearest subject. In the sentence above the nearest subject is "assistants."

    e. The verbs in who, which, and that clauses must agree in number with the word they depend upon:

EXAMPLES:

This is one of the many problems which have concerned us for many years.
(Which in this sentence depends on problems; therefore, it takes a plural verb.)

This is the only one of the topics which interests me.
(Which depends on one; therefore, it takes a singular verb.)

4. Whom do you want? The only area of our language that has retained a complete system of inflection (change of word form depending upon usage) is the pronoun formation.

These cause trouble mainly because we have dropped some forms in speech but have retained them in written English.

EXAMPLES:

It's me. (acceptable in speaking)
It is I. (the only really correct form in written English)
Who do you want? (natural and acceptable in speaking)
Whom do you want? (to be absolutely correct in written English)

    a. Perhaps the distinction between who and whom presents the most difficulty. The resistance to whom will likely cause it to be dropped from the language. Now, however, it is still very much with us, and writers should learn to use it correctly. Here is a simple test for deciding on who or whom: substitute he or him at the correct place in the sentence which calls for the use of who or whom.

EXAMPLES:

(1) He is a man whom you can trust.
Rearrange the sentence to read: You can trust him.
Therefore, whom is correct.

(2) Smith doesn't care whom he insults.
Rearrange: He insults him.
Therefore, whom is correct.

(3) Who do you think will write the report?
Rearrange (always change questions to statements):
You do think he will write the report.
Therefore, who is correct.

(4) Who did you say was to be chosen?
Rearrange (change question to statement):
You did say he was to be chosen.
Therefore, who is correct.

b. When a comparison using than or as calls for a pronoun after it, fill out the understood part of the sentence (the words within brackets in the examples below).

EXAMPLES:

(1) Give the report to Mr. Smith as well as [to] him.
(2) You know more about this matter than I [know].
(3) The regulation applies to part-time employees as well as [to] them.
(4) He was clearer in his presentation than I [was].

c. Pronoun choices following prepositions will take the object forms.

EXAMPLES:

(1) This matter is strictly between you and me.
(2) The briefing looked good to the chief and him.
(3) The funds are to be divided between you and him.

A simple test will usually guide you to the right choice of pronoun in sentences like those above: cross out all words between the preposition and the pronoun. Then read the sentence again.

EXAMPLES: (using the three sentences above):

7-12

(1) This matter is strictly between ~~you and~~ me.
(You would not say "between I," would you?)

(2) The briefing looked good to ~~the chief and~~ him.
(You would not say "to he," for it sounds odd.)

(3) The funds are to be divided between ~~you and~~ him.
(Again the phrase "between he" sounds quite incorrect.)

d. Following is a list of pronoun forms:

Subject (agent or actor)	Possessive (ownership)	Object (receiver of action)
I	my, mine	me
you	your, yours	you
he, she, it,	his, her, hers, its	him, her, it
we	our, ours	us
you	your, yours	you
they	their, theirs	them
who	whose	whom

5. <u>Have you forgotten the apostrophe?</u> The apostrophe has become a confusing mark principally because we have made it serve in three different areas:

 a. To show ownership (possessives). You will always be right if you follow these simple rules:

 (1) If the original word ended in "s," add an apostrophe.

 EXAMPLE: <u>James coat</u>. We are talking about a coat BELONGING TO <u>James</u>.

 Since the <u>original</u> word ended in "s," add an apostrophe--James' coat.

NOTE:

Some authors of textbooks will spend much time explaining that the possessive form James', for example, could also be spelled James's. This is a correct alternate form, but why bother cluttering your mind with unnecessary choices? Follow Rule (1) and you will <u>always</u> be right.

 (2) If the original word did not end in "s," add an apostrophe and an "s."

EXAMPLES:

<u>Mens</u> <u>coats</u>. We are talking about coats BELONGING TO the men. The word did not end in "s"; therefore, add 's--men's coats.

<u>An</u> <u>employees</u> <u>rights</u>. We are talking here about the rights BELONGING TO one employee. The word did not end in "s"; therefore, write--an employee's rights.*

*NOTE: While not true possessives, familiar expressions dealing with time or value also use the apostrophe. Check these using rules (1) and (2) above--did they end in "s" or not?

EXAMPLES: A week's pay, a moment's notice, two dollars' worth, a day's work, three hours' drive, today's paper.

b. To form contractions (shortened forms).

EXAMPLES:

cannot	-- can't
are not	-- aren't
will not	-- won't
of the clock	-- o'clock
the fall of 1898	-- the fall of '98

c. To show the plurals of words, letters and numbers pointed out as such in a sentence.

EXAMPLES:

The lawyer used five <u>whereas's</u> in this contract.
There are two <u>t's</u> in the word allotted.
There were two <u>64's</u> instead of one in the last column of figures.

CAUTION: Never use apostrophes with possessive pronouns (see list in 4.d. above). These are already inflected to show ownership:

WRONG: its', yours', hers', theirs', etc.
RIGHT: its, yours, hers, theirs, etc.

6. <u>Are</u> <u>you</u> <u>real</u> (or <u>really</u>) <u>confident</u> <u>about</u> <u>your</u> <u>English</u>? In the key sentence above the choice should have been <u>really</u> (adverb form) because it modifies a measuring word (adjective). Here it might be in order to review the functions of the adverb, the most complex part of speech in the language.

    a. The adverb may modify:

        (1) Verbs

            EXAMPLE: He was <u>really</u> skilled at that sport.

        (2) Another adverb

            EXAMPLE: The job was <u>really</u> quickly accomplished.

        (3) Adjectives

            EXAMPLE: He was <u>really</u> confident in his use of English after completing this training course.

    b. The adjective form (<u>real</u> in the above caption) modifies nouns or pronouns (naming words):

        EXAMPLE: He made a <u>real</u> attempt to succeed.

    c. Verbs of the "senses" need special consideration, for both adjectives and adverbs may modify them:

        (1) As modifiers of the subject (adjectives)

            EXAMPLES:

            ...The coffee tasted bitter.
            ...The weather turned cold.
            ...The chief looked angry.
            ...The air smells fresh.

            COMMENT: In all the sentences above, the word at the end adds a quality to (modifies) the subject. Also the "sense" verb in each sentence is a linking type and does not refer to an action of the subject. You can use two questions to test this type of sentence:

            ...Is the subject performing any action in the sentence? If not, choose an adjective form.

...Can you substitute <u>was</u> or <u>is</u> for the verb in the sentence? If you can, choose an adjective.

(2) But "sense" verbs when used as <u>action</u> verbs in the sentence are modified by adverbs:

EXAMPLES:

...He tasted the coffee cautiously.
...He turned directly up the hill.
...She looked carefully through the file.
...He smelled the container suspiciously, then notified the police.

COMMENT: In all the sentences under (2) above the test questions would reveal a different relationship:

...The verbs are action words indicating the subject doing something.

...You could not logically substitute <u>was</u> or <u>is</u> for the main verb.

RULE: If the subject is doing the action described and <u>was</u> or <u>is</u> could not replace the main verb, then the adverb form is correct.

7. <u>How about your signals</u> (punctuation)? Punctuation marks were invented as an aid to clarity. They should be considered functional not decorative and should be used only when you have a reason to justify their use. We will consider here only the most troublesome situations calling for punctuation.

a. Commas are the most often used marks and may appear singly or in pairs in the sentence. When commas are used at the beginning and end of part of the sentence, it is called "setting off" that element. Here are some typical uses of the comma:

(1) To set off parts of a sentence that are <u>not</u> <u>essential</u> to the basic meaning.

EXAMPLE: Colonel Smith, who is the Project Manager, will address the group.

NOTE: Do not punctuate around material <u>essential</u> to the meaning, as in this example:

The executive who has been named Project Manager will address the group.

ADDITIONAL EXAMPLES:

...And over here, my friends, you will see the reason for our trouble. (The phrase "my friends" could be dropped.)

...Mr. Smith, the Chief Accountant, will give the presentation. (His job title is not basically necessary to identify Mr. Smith as an individual.)

...Robert Gunning's *The Technique of Clear Writing* is a valuable reference book. (The title of the book is essential--don't punctuate around it.)

...Large corporations which award subcontracts help the smaller firms to succeed. (The "which" clause is needed to identify and limit "corporations"--don't punctuate around it.)

(2) To aid the clarity of the sentence.

EXAMPLES:

...Quoting the manager, Brown would be ideal for the assignment. (to avoid running the name together with "manager")

...If you wish, more can be done later. (comma prevents misreading)

(3) To separate introductory clauses, long phrases, and adverb modifiers.

EXAMPLES:

...Because the new contract offered benefits, the employees favored it.

...To the astonishment of all his subordinates, the manager resigned his position.

...Consequently, we present the following recommendations.

(4) To separate introductory verbal phrases from the rest of the sentence. Whenever an "ing" verb phrase is used at the beginning of a sentence, a comma follows it.

EXAMPLES:

...Considering your long and faithful service to the firm, we wish to present you the certificate.

...Having already related the main details of the project, I will now outline the specifics.

(5) To separate items in a series.

EXAMPLES:

...James, Brown, and Smith are eligible for the position.

...This officer is expected to interview applicants, to recommend the best suited, and to supervise personnel record-keeping.

b. The semicolon (;) is mainly used in double (compound) sentences. This usage was explained in the material under section C (p. 7-7) above: "Does your sentence go far enough or too far?"

EXAMPLE: ...Your report is complete; however, we will need additional support material.

c. The colon (:) is principally used to introduce a series in a sentence, a quotation, or a listing where symbols (1, 2, 3, or a, b, c,) are to be used:

EXAMPLES:

...The three requirements for the position are the following: a degree in nuclear engineering, a solid religious affiliation, and experience as a peanut farmer.

...Mark Twain once said: "The difference between the right word and the almost right word is like the difference between lightning and a lightning bug."

...We need these to continue the project:
1. Added personnel
2. More funding
3. Better laboratory facilities

NOTE: Omit using the colon in sentences where no general ("umbrella") term is used to introduce the series, such as the following, these, as follows, etc.

EXAMPLE: To succeed in politics you will need a lot of patience, a thick skin, and a few rich friends.

d. Dashes (--) are used singly or in pairs and can be used effectively to emphasize or strengthen ideas. Use the mark sparingly, however, by reserving its use for really important statements.

EXAMPLES:

...One thing is clear, gentlemen--our sales must increase.

...Our candidate has one message--return the government to the people--as the slogan of his campaign.

Whatever follows a dash or occurs between the two dashes will be highlighted for the reader.

e. Parentheses ( ) are always used in pairs. They enclose material that is not essential to the main thought of the sentence. Parentheses are used to under-emphasize ideas, to add material that is quite remote from the rest of the sentence. In their purpose, therefore, they contrast sharply with dashes.

EXAMPLES:

...We must secure sufficient funding (and we have mentioned this often) before proceeding with the plan.

...The presentation (the usual gimmicky approach) offered little of value.

NOTE: Of course, in the two sentences above the writer could have chosen to use dashes instead of parentheses. This would signal the reader that he wanted to call attention to the inserted remark.

f. Quotation marks " " (used always in pairs) enclose the exact words of the source.

> EXAMPLE: The boss said, "I want this completed by tomorrow noon."

> NOTE: Do not use quotation marks for indirect quotations.

> EXAMPLE: The boss said that he wanted this completed by tomorrow noon.

(1) Use single quotation marks <u>only</u> for quoting something occurring inside a larger quotation.

> EXAMPLE: The speaker said, "I have often quoted the phrase, 'Don't call me, I'll call you.'"

(2) Use of final quotation marks with other marks:

...The period and the comma <u>always</u> occur inside the final quotation mark.

> EXAMPLE: "I have clearly stated," the candidate continued, "my position on this issue."

...The colon and the semicolon <u>always</u> occur outside the final quotes.

> EXAMPLE: He announced, "We will pursue this matter thoroughly"; then he continued, "we will make a public disclosure of the facts."

...The question mark and exclamation mark are placed <u>inside</u> the final quotation mark when they apply only to the quoted matter; <u>outside</u> when they belong to the whole sentence.

> EXAMPLES:
>
> He asked, "What are the options?"
> Did he reply, "I have no idea"?

8. <u>How is your spelling?</u> Correct pronunciation of a word can be a guide to its correct spelling. If you give full value to all the syllables when you pronounce a word, you are more likely to spell it correctly. But because of the sometimes strange history of the English language, sound and spelling have often drifted far apart. For example, consider this amazing list of words all spelled differently but pronounced with the same <u>sh</u> sound:

7-20

shoe, sugar, issue, mansion, mission, nation, suspicion, ocean, nauseous, conscious, fuchsia, pshaw

English spelling is not, however, altogether chaotic. Some rules, such as the following, can be helpful:

a. Is it IE or EI? The familiar jingle will cover most words with the ie or ei combination: I before E, except after C or when pronounced as AY, as in neighbor and weigh.

EXAMPLES:

(1) i before e--achieve, believe, chief, grief, niece, relieve
(2) e before i--ceiling, conceited, conceive, perceive, receipt
(3) e before i (with AY sound)--eighty, vein, sleigh, freight

EXCEPTIONS: either, neither, leisure, seize, weird

b. Final silent e.

(1) Drop the final e before adding an ending (suffix) beginning with a vowel.

EXAMPLES: shine--shining
           judge--judging

(2) Retain the final e before adding an ending (suffix) beginning with a consonant.

EXAMPLES: require--requirement
           arrange--arrangement
           achieve--achievement
           sincere--sincerely

EXCEPTIONS: Retain the final e after a "soft" c or g (notice--noticeable, courage--courageous). Second, retain the final e to avoid confusion with other words (singe--singeing, compare with singing). Third, retain the e to prevent a mispronunciation (shoeing, not shoing).

c. Final Y.

(1) In adding endings to words change the y to an i when it follows a consonant.

7-21

EXAMPLES: bury--burial
noisy--noisily
beauty--beautiful

(2) Keep the y when it follows a vowel, when adding the -ing ending, or to form the plurals of proper names.

EXAMPLES: delay--delays, valley--valleys, play--played (final y follows a vowel)

bury--burying, cry--crying, try--trying (adding an -ing ending)

Brown--Browns, Daley--Daleys (proper names--note that the apostrophe is not used with the plural form of the name)

d. Doubling final consonants. This rule is quite complicated and may be too complex to be really useful. But if you can remember all of the following conditions for doubling the final consonant, you will be able to spell a whole set of words correctly:

(1) In one-syllable words double the final consonant when it is preceded by a single vowel, as in bar--barred, hop--hopping, slip--slipping. But when two vowels or another consonant precede the final consonant, do not double the consonant, as in stoop--stooped, dent--dented.
(two vowels)   (another consonant)

(2) In words of more than one syllable, double the final consonant when a single vowel precedes and the stress (accent) falls on the last syllable of the base word, as in admit--admitted, begin--beginning. But do not double the final consonant when the stress falls on other than the last syllable after the ending is added, or when the final consonant is preceded by two vowels, as in prefer--preference, repair--repairing.   (stress shifts)
(two vowels precede)
It is complicated, isn't it?

e. Adding prefixes. When adding prefixes such as dis-, mis-, de-, un-, retain the original spelling of the word-- do not drop or add any letters, as in dissimilar, misstate, de-emphasize, unnecessary.

Improving your spelling has to become an individual responsibility. Make a list of the words you consistently misspell. Look at the list from time to time and try to visualize the words. Look at a word in the list, then shut your eyes and try to see the word mentally. If you do this often enough, you will learn to spell it correctly.

F. <u>Words Commonly Confused</u>

Many English words are similar to each other in form and spelling. Note the distinctions among words in the following list:

1. Accept -- means "to receive"
   Except -- means "to exclude, leave out"

2. Adapt (verb) -- means "to adjust to a new situation"
   Adept (adjective) -- means "highly skilled, having dexterity"
   Adopt (verb) -- means "to take as one's own"

3. Adherence -- refers to "one's loyalty to a commitment"
   Adhesion -- refers to "things being stuck together"

4. Advice (noun) -- means "opinion given" or "suggestion"
   Advise (verb) -- means "to give advice"

5. Affect (verb) -- means "to influence"
   Effect (verb) -- means "to bring about"
   Effect (noun) -- means "the result"

6. Allude -- means "to make an indirect reference"
   Elude -- means "to escape detection"

7. Allusion -- means "a reference"
   Illusion -- means "an unreal or imaginary impression"

8. Already (adverb) -- means "before some designated time"
   All ready (adjective phrase) -- means "everyone or everything prepared for action

9. Altogether -- means "completely" or "thoroughly"
   All together -- means "the whole group" or "collected in one place"

10. Amount of -- refers to things measured in quantity or bulk
    Number of -- refers to separate items that may be counted

11. Ante- (prefix) -- means "before" or "in front of"
    Anti- (prefix) -- means "against" or "opposed to"

12. Approve -- means "to give official sanction to"
    Concur -- means "to agree with"

13. Ascent -- means "to rise"
    Assent -- means "agreement"

14. Augment -- means "to make greater, as in size, quantity, or strength"
    Supplement -- means "to add to in order to make up something lacking"

15. Average -- refers to "an arithmetical *mean*, arrived at by dividing a sum or two or more quantities by the number of quantities"
    Median -- refers to "the middle number in a sequence of numbers"

16. Bare (adjective) -- means "unclothed" or "revealed"
    Bear (verb) -- means "to carry," "put up with," or "give birth to"
    Bear (noun) -- means "an animal"

17. Beside -- means "at the side of"
    Besides -- means "in addition to"

18. Between -- used to refer to *two* persons or events
    Among -- used to refer to *three* or more persons or events

19. Bi- (prefix) -- means "multiplied by two"
    Semi- (prefix) -- means "divided by two"

20. Brake -- means "to slow down"
    Break -- means "to destroy"

21. Capital -- refers either "to wealth" or "to the city containing the seat of government of a state or nation"
    Capitol -- refers to a "building where a governmental body meets"

22. Censor -- means "to examine in order to note and omit objectionable material"
    Censure -- means "to criticize or blame"

23. Cite -- means "to refer to"
    Site -- means "a place"
    Sight -- means "what one sees"

24. Compare -- usually means "to consider in a way to show both likenesses and differences"
    Contrast -- means "to consider only to show differences"

25. Complement (noun or verb) -- means "anything that completes a whole"
    Compliment (noun or verb) -- means "a term of praise or the act of praising"

26. Concept -- refers to "a thought or an idea"
    Conception -- refers to "the larger sum of a person's impressions on a subject"

27. Continual -- refers to "events occurring often enough to be considered a series"
    Continuous -- refers to "an action that occurs without interruption"

28. Credible -- means "capable of being believed"

    Creditable -- means "worthy of praise or recognition"
    Credulous -- means "gullible, willing to believe on insufficient evidence"

29. Descent -- means "to go down"
    Dissent -- means "to disagree"

30. Desert (verb) -- means "to leave"
    Desert (noun) -- means "a dry place"
    Dessert (noun) -- means "an after dinner dish"

31. Diagnosis -- means "the conclusion reached by investigation"
    Prognosis -- means "a forecast or a prediction"

32. Direct (adjective) -- means "straight" or "through no one else"
    Directly (adverb) -- means "in a short time"

33. Discreet -- means "careful, respectful"
    Discrete -- means "distinct, considered individually"

34. Disinterested -- means "impartial, unbiased"
    Uninterested -- means "having no interest in"

35. Economic -- means "pertaining to the production, distribution, and consumption of material wealth"
    Economical -- means "not wasteful or extravagant"

36. Elicit -- means "to bring out"
    Illicit -- means "illegal"

37. Emigrate -- means "to leave one place (usually a country) for another"
    Immigrate -- means "to come into a country from another"

38. Eminent -- means "outstanding" or "of high importance"
    Imminent -- means "about to happen"
    Immanent -- means "existing within, inherent"

39. Enormity -- means "great wickedness, an outrageous act"
    Enormousness -- means "great in size"

40. Explicit -- means "something expressed precisely and directly"
    Implicit -- means "an idea found within a statement but not directly expressed"

41. Fair -- means ""average" or "pretty"
    Fare -- means "a charge for transportation"

42. Famous -- means "well-known for good reasons"
    Infamous ⎤
    Notorious ⎦ -- both mean "well-known but unfavorably regarded"

43. Farther -- preferred to express meaning of "measurable distance"
    Further -- preferred to mean "a greater degree" or "more"

44. Fewer -- used to refer to items that can be counted
    Less -- used to refer to quantity or bulk amounts

45. Figuratively -- means "not actual but presented as a figure of speech"
    Literally -- refers to "something actual and real"

46. Flammable ⎤
    Inflammable ⎦ -- both refer to "substances that will burn"
    Non-flammable -- means "something that will not burn"

47. Flaunt -- means "to make a showy display of"
    Flout -- means "to show scorn for"

48. Formally -- means "following custom or rules"
    Formerly -- means "previously"

49. Hanged -- means "to execute" (legal term)
    Hung -- means "to place, suspend"

50. Healthy -- refers to "something or someone that has good health"
    Healthful -- refers to "a substance that gives health"

51. Historic -- refers to "a place or event of importance in history"
    Historical -- refers to "any event that has occurred in the past, important or not"

52. Imply -- means "to hint or suggest"
    Infer -- means "to arrive at by reasoning"

53. Incredible -- means "unbelievable, unreal"
    Incredulous -- means "skeptical, doubting"

54. Ingenious -- means "highly skilled" or "very clever"
    Ingenuous -- means "showing innocent or childlike simplicity"

55. Its -- is the possessive form of "it"
    It's -- always means "it is"

56. Lead (verb) -- means "to conduct, direct"
    Lead (noun) -- refers to the metal
    Led (verb form) -- is the past tense or participle of the verb "lead"

57. Lend (used only as a verb) -- means "to give temporarily"
    Loan (noun) -- means "something given"
    Loan (verb) -- means also "to give temporarily"

58. Lessen -- means "to make easier or fewer"
    Lesson -- means "something learned"

59. Loose (verb) -- means "to free, unfasten, let go"
    Loose (adjective) -- means "unrestrained, unconfined"
    Lose (verb) -- means "to misplace" or "to reduce in amount"

60. Majority -- means "more than half of the total (in elections more than half of the total votes cast)"
    Plurality -- means "the excess number received over the next highest (in elections with three or more candidates, the number of votes received over the next highest)"

61. Notable -- refers to "something worthy of notice, important"
    Noticeable -- refers to "something apparent enough to be noticed"

62. Observance -- refers to "following of a custom, tradition, law, duty, etc."
    Observation -- means "the act of noticing something"

63. Passed (verb--past tense of pass) -- means "gone beyond" or "successfully attained"
    Past (noun) -- means "a previous time"

64. Personal (adjective) -- means "referring to a person"
    Personnel (noun) -- refers to a "group of people concerned with a common project"

65. Plane -- means "a carpentry tool" or "an airborne vehicle"
    Plain -- means "clear" or "not decorative"

66. Practical -- means "sensible, useful, not theoretical"
    Practicable -- means "feasible, capable of being put into practice"

67. Presence -- means "in attendance"
    Presents -- means "gifts"

68. Principal -- means "chief, main, head" -- also "an amount of money"
    Principle -- means "a truth, a standard for action, a rule"

69. Quite -- means "completely" or "positively"
    Quiet -- means "absence of noise, calm, unmoving"

70. Raise -- means "to build up"
    Raze -- means "to tear down"

71. Scene -- means "what one sees"
    Seen (past participle of see) -- means "observed"

72. Tenant -- refers to "one occupying a piece of property"
    Tenet -- means "an opinion or belief held by someone"

73. Then -- means "at that time"
    Than -- means "a term of comparison"

74. There -- a "pointer" word meaning "in a certain position"
    Their -- possessive form of they
    They're -- contraction for "they are"

75. Waist -- means "the middle of the body"
    Waste -- means "discarded material"

76. Wait on -- refers to "the services of waiters and waitresses"
    Wait for -- refers to "the time delay before an expected action"

Summary

In this chapter we have examined how the principles of language change and how levels of usage affect correctness. Then we isolated eight common usage problems and showed how to correct them.

Exercise 1   Chapter Seven   **FRAGMENT AND RUN-ON SENTENCES**

Directions: Correct the following sentences by revising the wording or by adding the correct punctuation:

1. The presentation was excellent the speaker received an enthusiastic response.

2. Referring to your proposal concerning the bid on Project X.

3. The proposal has been examined and the data analyzed, however no action at this time is possible.

4. We have no alternative to suggest at this time. Having written two letters and received no response.

5. The employee that I told you about and recommended for the position.

6. The research has been completed therefore, we are ready to proceed with the plan.

7. We cannot exchange the article it is damaged.

8. Davis having testified before the Civil Aeronautics Board.

Exercise 1--page two

9. The Commission will examine the evidence and then it will render its decision.

10. The project will definitely be undertaken. The concurrence having been received.

Exercise 2   Chapter Seven   VERB TENSES

Directions: Change the verb forms in the following sentences to make the time reference correct:

1. If his report came earlier, the contract would not have been signed.

2. Mr. Smith will leave by the time this message reaches his office.

3. It is the same sound I had heard the day before.

4. Mr. Price couldn't explain why the previous owners move out so suddenly.

5. An ambulance arrived only ten minutes after the foreman reported the accident.

6. At the conference yesterday I noticed that you forgot your briefcase.

7. Since the supervisor leaves at noon, he has failed to see the report.

8. The dam bursted and flooded thousands of acres of farmland in the valley below.

9. We arrived at the meeting just in time for the opening speech. The first speaker talks about employee responsibilities.

Exercise 2--page two

10. By next month we will complete the initial plans for the new installation.

11. Yes, I often had that responsibility as part of my duties on my present job.

12. It was obvious to the investigator that the supervisor completely performed his mission.

13. All the employees agreed that the union represented them well.

14. I had been acting as the deputy before the Chief gives me another assignment.

Exercise 3   Chapter Seven   MATCHING SUBJECTS
                                                   AND VERBS

Directions: Circle the correct verb forms in the following
              sentences:

1. The report and the graph (was, were) missing.

2. The most valuable aspect of the conferences (was, were) the employee services presentation.

3. The Chief Accountant or his assistant (is, are) responsible for the monthly reports.

4. The training director or his staff members (conduct, conducts) the conferences.

5. The reason for the objections (concern, concerns) the possibilities of error in projecting costs.

6. Each of the members (sign, signs) up for a full year.

7. The manager, together with members of his staff, (is, are) to be congratulated on this success.

8. Neither the directors nor Mr. Davis (has, have) accepted the plan.

9. Neither Mr. Davis nor the directors (has, have) accepted the plan.

10. He demonstrated one of the plans that (was, were) successful for firms of our size.

11. This is the only procedure that (shows, show) promise of success.

12. Neither of my questions (has, have) been answered satisfactorily.

13. He ordered one of the desks that (was, were) on sale.

14. The Program Director, as well as his subordinates, (decides, decide) on the final plans.

15. This is one of those species that (is, are) very rare.

Exercise 4   Chapter Seven   CHOICE OF PRONOUN

Directions: Circle the right pronoun in these sentences:

1. Between you and (I, me) the assignment would be a challenge.

2. (Whoever, whomever) is working the night shift has that responsibility.

3. (We, us) small companies have a hard time competing for contracts.

4. Was it (they, them) (who, whom) the department has released from duty.

5. Did anybody inquire about Smith and (I, me)?

6. We have not yet determined (who, whom) will replace Smith.

7. The success of the project means a great deal to the supervisor and (I, me).

8. (Who, whom) generally is assigned to this job area?

9. My question is directed to (whoever, whomever) has the current data.

10. I'm sure that the supervisor and (I, me) were aware that it was (she, her) responsibility.

11. He maintains that the job requires an employee with more experience than (I, me.)

12. These statistics are disturbing to Mr. Davis as well as (I, me).

13. (We, us) businessmen must protest this latest tax bill.

14. The executives agreed to settle the matter between you and (I, me).

15. They demanded that these three appear--Smith, Jones, and (I, me).

Exercise 4--page two

17. The report does not seem to represent the best efforts of you and (I, me).

18. With (who, whom) have you checked about this difficulty?

19. Can you tell me (who, whom) will represent us at the meeting?

20. It is important to know (who, whom) this act will benefit.

Exercise 5　　　　　　　Chapter Seven　　　　　　APOSTROPHES

Directions:　Circle the right usage from the choices offered in the following sentences:

1. Mr. (Browns, Brown's, Browns') report is on the desk.

2. The data were carried in (todays, today's todays') <u>Business Review</u>.

3. A comparison of (their, there, they're) economy and (our's, ours, ours') reveals great differences.

4. This paper features "All the news (that's thats, thats') fit to print."

5. A few years later she joined Mr. (Harrimans, Harriman's, Harrimans') staff.

6. If the senate (committee's, committees', committees) bill is accepted, the law will be passed.

7. These names all begin with (A's, As', As).

8. The trouble with (one's, ones, ones') success is that (it's, its, its') unpredictable.

9. Will modern industrial waste pollute the (world's, worlds, worlds') atmosphere?

10. Our troops must know what (they're, their, there) fighting for.

11. The number of (and's, ands, ands') in the report made it confusing.

12. Put the file back in (it's, its', its) proper place.

13. He was forced to place someone else in his (son-in-law's, son-in-laws') position.

14. (What's, whats', whats) the main cause of all the difficulty?

15. We were surprised at (your, you're, your') refusing to join the group.

Exercise 6   Chapter Seven   ADJECTIVES AND ADVERBS

Directions: Circle the correct choice in the following sentences:

1. Suddenly he said that he felt (real, really) (bad, badly) and his face turned white.

2. The director looked (sharp, sharply) at me when I mentioned that problem.

3. The duplicator needs repairs (bad, badly).

4. The project was done on time and (efficient, efficiently).

5. He reported that the new director looks (capable, capably).

6. His secretary looked (careful, carefully) through the file for that important letter.

7. The casing of the gun felt (smooth, smoothly) to the inspector.

8. The accountant felt (miserable, miserably) over the large number of errors.

9. Since we installed air conditioning, the air in this office smells (fresh, freshly).

10. The Fire Chief smelled the partly burned material (cautious, cautiously).

11. The committee report somehow sounded (incomplete, incompletely) to me.

12. Weedos taste (good, well) like a cigarette should.

13. The lieutenant tasted the white powder (careful, carefully).

14. (Most, Almost) all property is readily identified in this way.

Exercise 7   Chapter Seven   PUNCTUATION

Directions: Circle the right mark in the places indicated in these sentences. "N" means that no punctuation should be used at that point in the sentence.

1. The manager (, N) who was first assigned to the project (, N) gave the briefing.

2. My supervisor (, N) who is also assigned to Personnel (, N) gave me the file.

3. In that corner (, N) as you will see (, N) is the Graphics Section.

4. Rudolph Flesch (, N) an expert on writing practice (, N) conducted the seminar.

5. The speaker (, N) whose subject was Effective Writing (, N) conducted the seminar.

6. Because the Acme Company made the lowest bid (, N) the committee accepted their contract.

7. Having seen the results of the study(, N) the Chief was pleased.

8. At the border (, N) inspectors will open all your luggage.

9. Your duties are as follows (, : N) supervise the accountants (, N) prepare monthly reports (, N) and present an annual briefing.

10. The employees are aware of that (, ; N) however (, ; N) the number of problems keep rising.

11. You will need (; N :) a thick skin, a soft heart, and a good head to succeed here.

7-39

Exercise 7--page two

12. The foreman shouted over the noise of the machinery (, N --) "Stop the presses!"

13. One thing is clear (: , --) Whatever is, is right.

14. The boss told me (, N) just at quitting time (, N) about the need to finish the job.

15. The speaker said (" N) that he had had twenty years experience with computer management. (" N)

16. He asked, (" N) Why start that just before your vacation ("? N ?")

17. Did they say, (" N) We are willing to undertake the job (?" "?)

18. (" N) Regardless of the consequences (," N ") he added (," N ",) we will continue to refer to that trip as a (' N ,) junket (.'" N ".")

19. (" N) First get the measurements of the laboratory (," N ",) he said (;" N ";) then we will submit a bid for the work to be done (". N .")

20. Jack said (" N ,") that he would be glad to represent out interests at the conference (." N .)

7-40

Exercise 8   Chapter Seven   WORDS COMMONLY
                                      CONFUSED

Directions: In the following sentences fill in the blanks with the correct choices from the words listed after each sentence. (In some sentences variant forms of the word listed should be used.)

1. _____ for my lack of background, I would have _____ the position. (accept, except)

2. The Agency will _____ a plan for locating _____ executives who will be able to _____ to new situations. (adept, adopt, adapt)

3. I tried to _____ him that he had received bad _____. (advice, advise)

4. The _____ of the policy _____ the workers' efficiency, and eventually a change was _____. (affect, effect)

5. Since he had an _____ that he was Napoleon, he made an _____ to French history. (allusion, illusion)

6. The crew was _____ at the launching pad before the equipment was _____ for the space shot. (already, all ready)

7. We were _____ in the conference room when the manager admitted that he was not _____ in favor of the change. (altogether, all together)

8. The _____ bushels of corn in storage determines the _____ the subsidy to be granted. (amount of, number of)

9. I will try to convince him to _____ with your proposal. Then perhaps the Project Manager will _____ the plans. (approve, concur.)

7-41

Exercise 8--page two

10. _____ his excellent credentials he presents superior personal qualifications for the position. (Beside, Besides)

11. _____ you and me the information has already been shared _____ the six directors. (Between, Among)

12. The _____ annual report is printed every six months. (bi-, semi-)

13. The Senator is subject to _____ for _____ his subordinates' mail. (censor, censure)

14. We ought to _____ the plans in order to _____ their differences. (compare, contrast)

15. The leak has caused a _____ flow of water since last Thursday. (continuous, continual)

16. He delivered a _____ argument, but I find his _____ attitude a real obstacle in the negotiations. (credible, credulous)

17. The report contained a thorough _____ of the history of this continuing problem. (diagnosis, prognosis)

18. The study should reach you _____; then you should forward it _____ to the Controller. (direct, directly)

19. The _____ war demonstrators occupied the _____ chamber to the President's office. (anti-, ante-)

20. The _____ number in this set -- 23-24-25-26-27-28-29-- is 26. (median, average)

21. The doctor suggested Vitamin B1 to _____ his diet. (augment, supplement)

22. The _____ Building is located in Des Moines, the _____ city. (capitol, capital)

23. A good judge ought to be _____ in the case being argued in his court. (uninterested, disinterested)

Exercise 8--page three

24. The group was told to _____ from England or face the consequences of the law. (immigrate, emigrate)

25. The _____ he got from home, the _____ in debt he went. (further, farther)

26. Those who _____ the law eventually have to pay for it. (flaunt, flout)

27. The criminal was _____ for his crime. (hanged, hung)

28. They were _____ on their fine performance as a fitting _____ to the program. (complement, compliment)

29. My _____ of the problem includes the _____ of a radical change. (concept, conception)

30. _____ progress can only be made by correspondingly _____ measures by the Government. (economic, economical)

31. An _____ scientist predicted that an earthquake was _____. (immanent, eminent, imminent)

32. The _____ of his crime was matched only by the _____ of his size. (enormity, enormousness)

33. I _____ from his remarks that he _____ a reduction in the staff. (implied, inferred)

34. The bus driver told the police an _____ story which left them _____. (incredible, incredulous)

35. The boss had to admit that the plan was clever enough to be termed _____. (ingenuous, ingenious)

7-43

Exercise 8--page four

36. Quality Control rejected the material because of _____ color. (its, it's, its')

37. The scout _____ them to a region where there were vast _____ deposits. (lead, led)

38. Please _____ me ten dollars so I can pay back a _____ I made last week. (lend, loan)

39. As soon as the _____ pully was repaired, the machine no longer continued to _____ oil. (loose, lose)

40. Of the three candidates Jones received a _____ of the votes but not a _____ of the total. (plurality, majority)

41. The speaker made the _____ that in most countries the _____ of anniversaries of historic events is common. (observance, observation)

42. The Director made a _____ reference when he spoke about the _____ practices in government employment. (personal, personnel)

43. A _____ plan is not always _____ when applied to actual shop procedure. (practical, practicable)

44. According to the _____ witness the teller absconded with the _____ as well as with the interest. (principal, principle)

45. It was _____ out of the question that the office could offer anyone peace and _____. (quiet, quite)

46. The _____ maintained that he couldn't be evicted because of the _____ that "possession is nine-tenths of the law." (tenet, tenant)

47. Over _____ in the corner _____ coats are piled up while _____ attending the class. (they're, their, there)

7-44

48. The police officer _____ to the clever means the convict took to _____ the "authorities." (elude, allude)

49. He was so _____ in the proceedings that he fell asleep. (disinterested, uninterested)

50. A substance that will not burn should be marked "_____." (flammable, inflammable, non-flammable)

51. The pilot's _____ to the change in flight plan, made the plane's _____ easier to manage. (assent, ascent)

52. What a _____ greeted our eyes as we reached the _____ of the camp! (cite, sight, site)

53. The police tried to _____ some answers about the _____ affair. (illicit, elicit)

54. _____ the prisoner gave a less-_____-acceptable explanation of his whereabouts that night. (than, then)

55. _____ planning to attend the meeting if _____ supplies get _____ on time. (there, their, they're)

Questions and/or Comments for Class Discussion

POSTSCRIPT

This instruction cannot guarantee to make you a successful writer. Nor can any course make that claim. The training has, however, suggested techniques to help you improve the quality and effectiveness of your writing. After the class sessions are over, try to work on the areas where you need the most help. Refer to the text and the exercises from time to time--this will encourage you to continue to improve your writing. And, as we have seen, the process is a never-ending one, even for the most gifted of professional writers.

The 5 C's Formula offers no miraculous cure for all writing ills. It does, however, point the way--the rest is up to you.

We began this textbook with the idea that the purpose of training and education is to bring about change in attitudes and methods. Let us end by citing once again Goethe's expression of this goal:

> If you treat a man as he is, he will remain as he is. If you treat him as if he were what he could and should be, he will become what he could and should be.

INDEX

A

Abstract terms 3-2, 3-3
Abstraction ladders 2-6, 2-7, 3-4
Abstraction process 2-5
Active voice 5-7
Ad Hominem (fallacy) 6-10
Ad verecundiam (fallacy) 6-8
Adjectives 7-15, 7-16
Adverbs 7-15, 7-16
"Agency" comparative 6-10
Analytical language 5-1
Apostrophes 7-13, 7-14
Argument to the Man (fallacy) 6-10
Argument to the People (fallacy) 6-9
Aristotle 5-17
Arranging an outline (in reports) 5-23
Attitude in Writing 1-2, 1-3
  Checklist 1-3

B

Bacon, Francis 5-14
Balanced construction 5-6
"Bandwagon" fallacy 6-9
Begging the Question (fallacy) 6-10
"Belief systems" 2-4
Breaking down sentence elements 4-6
Broad Generalization (fallacy) 6-8

C

Carroll, Lewis 5-2
Checklist (considerate expression) 6-13
Churchill, Winston 7-3
Clarity (final test for) 3-12
Clear writing 3-1 thru 3-24

C (cont.)

Clichés 3-9, 4-7, 4-13
  (list of) 4-13 thru 4-15
Coherence in the paragraph 5-10
Coherent writing 5-1 thru 5-43
Colons (use of) 7-18, 7-19
Combining ideas 5-9
Commas (use of) 7-16 thru 7-18
Common connotations 2-9
Common usage problems 7-6
Comparative modifiers 4-10
Comparison, illogical 6-10
Comparisons in sentences 5-7
Compound (double) sentences 7-7, 7-18
Concise writing 4-1 thru 4-25
Concrete terms 3-2
Conditional "if" clauses 6-7
Conditional verb forms 6-6
Connective words 5-3, 5-4, 5-6
Connotations 2-8, 2-9
  personal 2-9
  common 2-9
Considerate writing 6-1 thru 6-23
Contractions 7-14
Coordinating conjunctions 5-6
Correct writing 7-1 thru 7-46
Correlative conjunctions 5-6
Cowles, Gardner 4-3

D

Dashes (use of) 7-19
"Dead level" abstracting 3-3
Deadwood 4-10, 4-11
Deductive patterns (in reports) 5-14, 5-15, 5-17
Denotation 2-8
"Detente" 2-8
Developing main ideas (in reports) 5-22
Double (compound) sentences 7-7, 7-18
Double connectives 5-6
Doublets 4-9

E

Either...or fallacy 6-11
Equality connectives 5-6
Euphemisms 4-11, 4-12
Excessive subordination 5-5
"Executive" report 5-17, 5-18

F

Facts 2-10, 6-3, 6-4
"Fad" words 3-8, 3-9
Fallacies, logical 6-8 thru 6-11
Five "C's" 1-1, 3-1
"Five W's and H" pattern (in reports) 5-20
Fog Index 3-10, 3-11, 4-1
Formal English 7-4
Four steps (report development) 5-21
Fragment 7-6
Fulbright, William 2-8
Future Perfect tense 7-8, 7-9
Future tense 7-8, 7-9

G

General English 7-4
General purpose statement (in reports) 5-21, 5-22
General vs specific terms 3-4, 4-9
Goethe 1-1
Gunning, Robert 3-10

H

Hasty Generalization (fallacy) 6-8
Hedgers 6-7, 6-8

I

"I" attitude 2-4, 6-1, 6-3
"Idea" world 2-2, 2-3
Illogical comparisons 6-10
Image-making level 2-3

I (cont.)

Impressive words (list of) 4-4
Indefinite words 4-7
Inductive patterns (in reports) 5-15, 5-16, 5-17
Inferences 2-7, 2-10, 6-3, 6-4
Inflated language 4-11
Informal English 7-5
Intensives 6-7
Introduction-Body-Conclusion order (in reports) 5-14, 5-17
Inversion 5-3
"It is" construction 4-7
Items in a series 5-6, 5-7

J

Jargon 3-6, 3-7
Johnson, Samuel 4-12
Judgments 2-10, 6-3, 6-5

K

Keats, John 2-9
Kitzhaber, Albert 1-5

L

Levels of usage 7-4
    Formal 7-4
    General 7-4
    Informal 7-5
    Vulgate 7-5
Lewis, Sinclair 1-7
Lincoln, Abraham 2-12
Logical fallacies 6-8 thru 6-11

M

McCarthy, Joe 2-8
"Mapping" 2-5
Matching subject and verb 7-10, 7-11
Middle sentences (in paragraphs) 5-11

N

"Narrowing" 2-5
Negative Expression 6-11, 6-12
Neologisms 3-8, 3-9
Neutral language 2-10
Nichols, Ralph 1-4
Non-sequitur (fallacy) 6-9
Non-verbal level 2-3, 2-4
Nouns as modifiers 4-11

O

Objective writing 2-10
Organizational patterns
   (in reports) 5-14, 5-19
Outlining 1-6
   Exercise 1-13
Outlining (in reports)
   5-23, 5-24

P

Paine, Tom 4-5
Paragraph coherence 5-10
Parallel structure 5-6
Parentheses (use of) 7-19
Passive voice 5-7
Past Perfect tense 7-8, 7-9
Past tense 7-8, 7-9
Patterns of coherence
   (in reports) 5-14
Personal connotations 2-9
Personal judgments 6-6
Persuasive Writing (steps in)
   5-17
Pointer words (in paragraphs)
   5-11, 5-12
Pope, Alexander 4-1, 7-1
"Position" language 5-1, 5-2
Positive expression 6-11
Post hoc, ergo propter hoc
   (fallacy) 6-9
Prepositional phrases 4-7
   (list of) 4-8 and 4-9
Present Perfect tense 7-8, 7-9
Present tense 7-8, 7-9
Primary tenses 7-8

P (cont.)

Pronoun choices 7-11 thru 7-13
   (list of) 7-13
Pronouns (use of in paragraphs)
   5-11, 5-12
Punctuation 7-16
   commas 7-16 thru 7-18
   semicolons 7-7, 7-18
   colons 7-18, 7-19
   parentheses 7-19
   dashes 7-19
   quotation marks 7-20
Purist view of language 7-1,
   7-2
Purpose 1-2, 1-3, 2-3
Purpose (aid to clarity) 3-5
Purpose statement (in reports)
   5-21
   general 5-21
   specific 5-22

Q

Quotation marks (use of) 7-20

R

Readability formulas 3-10 thru
   3-12
"Real" world 2-2, 2-3
Redundancy 4-9
   "doublets" 4-9
   general-specific terms 4-9
   comparative modifiers 4-10
   repetition 4-10
   deadwood 4-10, 4-11
"Relative" words 6-13
Repeated words (in paragraphs)
   5-11, 5-12
Repetition in writing 4-10,
   4-11
Revising drafts 1-7
Run-on sentences 7-7

S

Sample report 5-24 thru 5-27
"Sandwich" paragraph 5-10, 5-11
Secondary tenses 7-8

S (cont.)

Semicolon (use of) 7-7, 7-18
"Sense" verbs 7-15, 7-16
Sentence units (order of) 5-2, 5-3
Series (use of in sentences) 5-6, 5-7
Shakespeare, William 7-3
Short words 4-3, 4-4
Simple words 4-4
Slanting 2-11
Space order (in reports) 5-14, 5-16
Specific purpose statement (in reports) 5-22
Specific terms 3-4
Speed writing 1-4
Spelling rules 7-20 thru 7-23
    ie or ei 7-21
    final silent e 7-21
    final y 7-21, 7-22
    doubling final consonants 7-22
    adding prefixes 7-22
Standard progress report 3-22
Stereotyping 2-4, 2-5
Strunk, William 7-2
Subject-Verb-Object order 5-5
Subordination of ideas 5-5
Summary sentences 5-10, 5-11
Swift, Jonathan 6-4
Symbols 2-11

T

Technique of Clear Writing 3-10
Time order (in reports) 5-14, 5-15
Topic sentence 5-10, 5-11
Transfer Device (fallacy) 6-8
Transitional paragraph 3-13, 5-13, 5-14
Transition words (in paragraphs) 5-12,
    (list of) 5-12, 5-13

V

Value judgments 6-5
Variety in sentence arrangement 5-8, 5-9
Variety in sentence length 5-8
Verb tenses 7-8 thru 7-10
Verbal connectives (in paragraphs) 5-11, 5-12
Verbal level 2-2, 2-3, 2-4
Verbiage 4-2, 4-6, 4-7
Voltaire 4-6
Vulgate English 7-5

W

"Weasel-wording" 6-7
"Which Hunts" 4-6
Who (use of) 7-11 thru 7-13
Whom (use of) 7-11 thru 7-13
"Word" world 2-2, 2-3
Words Commonly Confused 7-23 thru 7-29
"Working" verbs 4-4, 4-5
Writing from an outline (in reports) 5-23, 5-24
Writing inventory (exercise) 1-8
Writing method (exercise) 1-11
Writing process, steps in 1-6, 1-7

Y

"YOU" attitude 2-4, 5-7, 6-1 thru 6-3

Acknowledgements

1. For the quotation on page 1-4:

   Ralph G. Nichols, "Listening Is Good Business."
   Ann Arbor, Michigan, Bureau of Industrial Relations,
   The University of Michigan, 1961. Used by permission.

2. For use of the Fog Index Formula quoted on pages 3-10 and 3-11:

   Adapted from Robert Gunning, <u>The Technique of Clear Writing</u>.
   New York, McGraw-Hill, revised edition, 1968. Copyright 1979
   by Gunning-Mueller Clear Writing Institute, Inc., Santa
   Barbara, California. Used by permission.

****

Special thanks are due to the following:

1. The St. Ambrose College Administration for granting the author a sabbatical leave in 1983 to prepare the text.

2. The Word-Processing staff at St. Ambrose College for their diligent work in preparing the manuscript.

3. Kathleen McInerney for proof-reading the manuscript.

4. Many hundreds of students who have contributed significantly to the author's education.

PE 1479 .B87 M37